BEYOND THE
COLLECTION PLATE

MICHAEL DURALL

Beyond the Collection Plate

Overcoming Obstacles
to Faithful Giving

Abingdon Press
Nashville

BEYOND THE COLLECTION PLATE
OVERCOMING OBSTACLES TO FAITHFUL GIVING

Copyright © 2003 by Abingdon Press

This book is printed on recycled, acid-free, elemental-chlorine–free paper.

Library of Congress Cataloging-in-Publication Data

Durall, Michael.
  Beyond the collection plate : overcoming obstacles to faithful giving
/ Michael Durall.
    p. cm.
Includes bibliographical references.
  ISBN 0-687-02315-7 (alk. paper)
  1. Church finance. I. Title.

BV770D87 2003
254'.8--dc21

2003004945

03 04 05 06 07 08 09 10 11 12 —10 9 8 7 6 5 4 3 2 1

MANUFACTURED IN THE UNITED STATES OF AMERICA

To my wife Diane,
without whom this book would
never have been possible, and to
clergy, lay leaders, and people in
the pews who strive mightily to
create vital and engaging
congregations

Contents

Foreword

The reason this book will be so valuable to you is that it approaches the whole issue of money and the church in the right way. If the secular world had indeed triumphed in North America, as so many people predicted in the 1960s, then the challenge to the church would have been "How can we *raise* money?" In fact, the secular world has largely disappeared in North America, lost in a bubbling cauldron of spirituality in which Christianity is now just a "small potato." In the world as it exists after 2000, the real question the church must answer is "How will we *use* money?" Raising money for spiritual purposes is really not a big problem. Using money wisely and effectively, so that spiritually motivated and ethically minded people will give you *more*, now *that* is the challenge!

The effective memory of most churches about stewardship goes back no further than the 1940s and 1950s. In those days, stewardship was simply about fund-raising. The credibility of religious institutions was not in doubt, so the only challenge was to invent marketing and accounting tactics to collect it. Then the credibility of religious institutions evaporated, religious leaders became increasingly embarrassed about being religious, and the definition of "stewardship" was broadened to encompass the philanthropic impulse itself (whether or not it was associated with any clear acquaintance with God). Moral people were encouraged to use their resources to "take care of" the whole world and every aspect of it. As as result:

• Church people came to believe that as long as their *attitude* was fundamentally "generous," "inclusive," and "friendly" they could justifiably limit their actual financial contributions to the church to percentage-giving measured in small single digits.

• Church people came to believe that their job was to sacrificially "take care of" God's world, rather than fulfill their destinies by "taking their place" in God's mission.

Philanthropy is big business in North America today, but churches do not *expect* their institutions to be competitive for the charitable dollar. Church operating budgets to maintain properties, salaries, pious music, and comfort food are subsidized, but mission budgets that demand spiritual disciplines and alternative lifestyles for members, and make magnanimous gestures to nonmembers are underfunded.

Michael Durall understands this profound missional fog in which the church today finds itself. Certainly he will coach you to raise money. More than this, he will coach you to use that money *wisely* (credibly, spiritually, and responsibly), and *effectively* (missionally, faithfully, and creatively). When the spiritually yearning, results-oriented public sees a deeply spiritual Christian community powerfully blessing the microcultures beyond its walls, they react in a predictable fashion. They give you *more money* and *more volunteer energy* that in turn generates *more volunteer energy* and *more money*.

Let me set the stage for Michael's practical and theoretical coaching. Here is the revolution in stewardship that separates the declining church from the thriving church.

In the world of declining church philanthropy that we are leaving behind, people within and beyond the church were motivated to give money by the following questions:

• Is there a project worth doing?
• Is there a program worth supporting?

Secular media or ecclesiastical marketing would reveal a crisis demanding a solution, a demographic requiring aid, an opportunity begging to be addressed, or an aging heritage deserving to be preserved. The church would reveal the program, design the strategic plan, and broker the infrastructure to get the job done. People would give the money, pray for its success, and go home to lunch confident in eventual victory. Yet the victory did not happen, the infrastructure became too expensive, the brokers proved unworthy, and people turned to wiser and more efficient organizations to do all the good they sincerely wanted to do.

In the world of thriving church faithfulness that is emerging, people within and beyond the church are motivated to give money by different questions:

- Do we have a faith worth sharing?
- Is there a spiritual leader worth following?

The first question leads people inward rather than outward. The foundation of all charity is the discernment that you, as an individual or as a congregation, have something of inestimable value that gives you hope for tomorrow and provides you with the confidence not to commit suicide tonight. If you share it you can give abundant life away to another person, and if you withhold it you risk abandoning another person to cruel fate. The second question leads people to decide whom they really trust. True charity is not about financially supporting a program, but trusting credible leaders to share the secret of abundant life with others and empower them to enjoy it.

The decision postmodern people make to invest their charitable dollars will be determined by their own conviction about grace and hopefulness about the future. The amount that postmodern people are ready to risk will be determined by how trustworthy a leader is to honor that grace and share that hope.

In the world of declining church philanthropy that we are leaving behind, people within and beyond the church make the following assumptions: God requires many sacrifices of my time, talent, and money; but fundamentally my lifestyle and God's mission are different things. Secular media and ecclesiastical preaching make it clear that charity should hurt. Generosity should not be joyous or fulfilling or rewarding; it should require careful negotiation between my preferences and God's preferences so that giving is neither too easy nor too hard. It is not just a belief that my needs should come first (my tastes, my family concerns, my health issues), nor even that our needs should come first (our church property maintenance, our harmony, our traditional music), but that these self-serving needs are *legitimately distinct* from whatever God happens to be "about" this year.

In the world of thriving church faithfulness that is emerging, people within and beyond the church make different assumptions: God requires only one sacrifice—myself—and therefore, my lifestyle and God's mission are one. The real issue is not whether I am willing to give up my life to acknowledge Jesus, but whether I am willing to give up my lifestyle to follow Jesus. As our neighborhood and that culture merge in the global village; as work, play, and leisure merge in the daily routine; as individuals, families, friends, and communities merge in holistic health; and as the infinite and the finite merge in a ferment of spirituality, my concerns and your concerns merge into God's concerns. The resulting urgency makes the budget lines for our church property, our worship harmony, and our traditional music look rather petty.

The choices postmodern people make to invest their charitable dollars will be determined by the potential to shape their lifestyles around a worthy cause. If the cause is big enough, bold enough, and biblical enough, they will give it everything they have.

This book is going to help you understand this emerging world and operate a thriving church that will deserve the trust of the public, walk with Jesus into mission, and make a positive difference in the world.

Thomas G. Bandy

Acknowledgments

I have been assisted in great measure by many people in writing this book. Chief among them is my friend and colleague Jeff Bradley, who encouraged me to begin writing in the first place.

Thomas Bandy ranks high on the list of those offering encouragement and sound advice. Thanks also to Jim Short and Cathy Bone, Marjie Fine, Michael Reeves, John Payne, Beth Banks, Norm Enfield, Robert Hoffman, Cecelia Kingman-Miller, Silvio Nardoni, Greg Meyer, Randy Boone, and members of The First Church in San Francisco and the Northwest Congregation in Atlanta for reading chapters of the book in draft form.

We have all the levels of economic status and we've had a lot of people without work. But there's never been a need, in these 25 years that I've been here, that I couldn't pick up a telephone to fulfill. The gifts are there; the gifts are always there. People are so willing to give; they just want to be asked.

Wilda Babineaux, St. Jules Catholic Church,
Lafayette, Louisiana[1]

Introduction

The purpose of this book is to convince clergy and lay leaders that there is plenty of money out there to create healthy and vital churches that can serve in ever greater ways. Church leaders often do not realize this, however, and struggle year after year to raise enough money to meet the budget and pay the church's bills.

Raising money is a central issue for any congregation. Equally important is what a church does with money once it is gathered in. This book addresses that essential and often overlooked subject. A major theme of this book is that a church's spending habits constitute an integral part of its discipleship.

For better or worse, issues involving money and stewardship play a critical role in the ability of any congregation to fulfill its mission and calling.

This book challenges a number of long-held assumptions about money that are often found in church. Chief among these assumptions are stewardship and financial practices implemented long ago that became ineffective over time, but are carried forward for no reason other than habit.

Churches raise money, spend money, and save money in varying proportions and amounts. Some congregations are generous with the resources they have, and seek opportunities to reach out to a world in need. Other churches, even some with sizable assets, exhibit a mentality that borders on miserliness.

Some churches display an acute anxiety about money, while others are confident that if the Lord calls, the Lord will provide. Some churches save large amounts of money for "rainy days" that may never come. Other churches prohibit the accumulation of funds, believing that God's work should be done here and now. How do churches arrive at such dramatically different perspectives? We'll explore these subjects in the pages to come.

An additional theme of this book is the role that clergy and lay leaders play in the financial affairs of the church. All too often, church leaders inherit long-held customs and traditions that may not serve the church well, but can be extremely difficult to change. When attempting to change the standing order, church leaders may find themselves subject to harsh criticism—sometimes from people who are less knowledgeable about the issues at hand, but who hold strong emotional views.

This book will point out potentially volatile issues that church leaders are likely to encounter, and offer suggestions about how to deflect criticism. Throughout the book, we'll discuss various forms of resistance to new ways of doing things at church. One of my goals is to build hope and confidence in church leaders, and to address those aspects of church life that create doubt and uncertainty in leadership. We'll also discuss the many rewards for leaders who create vital and engaging congregations.

People in the Pews

Beyond the institution of the church, we'll take a look at the lives of churchgoers today and their attitudes toward money in general. For example, parishioners are encouraged to heed passages in Scripture that exemplify charitable giving as one of our highest callings and noblest deeds. Regrettably, these words and phrases may motivate fewer and fewer people to support the church today. In many congregations, low-level and same-level giving is the norm. Established giving patterns are often deeply ingrained in the culture of church communities.

Congregants are certainly aware of Jesus' familiar words, "It is easier for a camel to go through the eye of a needle than for someone who is rich to enter the kingdom of God" (Mark 10:25). They also appear thoughtful while listening to appeals from the pulpit, or references to charitable giving as one of the hallmarks of a life well lived.

Yet when the pledge drive comes around, most people will give about the same amount as the previous year—or the previous five or ten years. What they heard has had little impact on what they give. The dedicated souls who led the pledge drive may wonder if their hard work has made much difference at all.

Another goal of this book is to help churches forge a strong and powerful bond between charitable giving and the day-to-day lives of parishioners. Giving is the nature of God. Churches must become more effective in helping their members live out this important premise.

This book differs from traditional stewardship literature in a number of ways. While the subject is money, this is not a "how to" book of fundraising techniques. Nonetheless, a major theme is the human need to give, both of our resources and ourselves. In doing so, we strive to create meaningful lives and become the kind of people God wants us to become.

Changing the behavior of parishioners in regard to how they spend money will not be an easy task. Princeton University professor Robert Wuthnow writes, "Money and material goods have us firmly in their grasp, but . . . we are painfully reluctant to admit this fact to ourselves." He goes on to say that "our worries about being too materialistic seem not to prevent us from wanting wealth."[1]

The "good life" in America, in the eyes of churchgoers and non-churchgoers alike, often means spacious homes, material objects, good food and drink, entertainment, travel, and all that our consumer society offers. I believe it is imperative for churches to redefine what the good life truly means.

Churches should call their members to lead lives of dedication, commitment, and sometimes even sacrifice. This is the good life. In order to create communities of faith that make a difference in the world and that set an example for our children and the generations to come, churches must challenge their members to lead lives that go against the grain of the prevailing consumer culture. Have we indeed gained the world, but lost our souls?

No Two Are Alike

This book also takes into account the uniqueness of individual congregations. Churches are endlessly fascinating because no two are quite alike. Churches just down the street from one another in the same town can vary dramatically in history, tradition, character, theology, and liturgy—and how they use the resources at their command.

Churches devise particular ways they deal with money, for better or worse. The people who make financial decisions, their personalities, and their attitudes toward money are key factors in each congregation. Thus, each church has what I refer to as a "financial identity."

I focus on discerning this identity in my work with congregations. Once determined, the financial identity of a congregation forms the basis of a tailor-made stewardship and financial plan. Since no two churches are alike, no two plans are alike. Some plans are relatively simple, while others are extremely complex. This book will help clergy and lay leaders define their church's financial identity and devise stewardship and financial plans accordingly.

This book is for clergy, lay leaders, and people in the pews who rise to the occasion when called—dedicated souls who are an inspiration to us all. Of course, everyone has this potential. Aren't churches here to help us achieve that?

CHAPTER ONE

Attitudes Toward Money in Church, Alas

People no longer give to the church simply because it is the church.

George Barna [1]

I often ask ministers and lay leaders to define the "mind-set" or culture of money in their congregations. Their responses are thoughtful, insightful, and all too often, sorrowful. In reviewing hundreds of responses from church leaders, a number of common patterns emerge. These are

—A reluctance to discuss financial matters openly, along with secrecy surrounding the amounts that parishioners contribute.

—Confusion about appropriate levels of giving, with suspicion that some give generously but many are stingy.

—A myth of scarcity, even in affluent congregations.

—Disbelief that there is full disclosure about income and expenses.

—Lack of agreement about proper use of the endowment.

—Conflicting attitudes that may disclose generational and/or theological differences between old and new members.

—Uncertainty among church leaders about how best to use funds the church has available.

—A lack of understanding about how charitable giving strengthens or enhances our spiritual lives.

Whatever their theology, congregations of all sizes can achieve worthwhile goals both great and small. It doesn't take a lot of money to create vital ministries, and churches with the most money do not always accomplish the greatest good. Nevertheless, the ebb and flow of money has a significant influence on a congregation's health, vitality, sense of worth, and confidence in achieving what God is calling it to do—and in helping its members lead lives of faith.

Summarized below is an array of quotations from clergy and lay leaders that define the culture of money in their congregations. Included are heartrending examples that reflect the financial struggles of many churches today, especially mainline congregations. An important goal in this book is to overcome these common difficulties. Other examples inspire, offer insight into effective ministry, and serve as beacons for us all.

Magical thinking would describe our approach to money. We think it will just appear, and we don't talk about it.

We have a horrible reluctance to spend money. The annual pledge drive is a time of high anxiety and tension.

We are not daring in our church life. We have trouble doing anything big. The congregation gives grudgingly.

We struggle with very low giving. People want to fall back on the endowment.

A lack of communication had resulted in a distrust of financial decisions made by the board, but we've begun to change that.

My church expects committees not to spend their budgets, to carry the church through. What kind of policy is that?

Thankfully, my church is moving to an attitude of "let's get it done" rather than "we don't have the money." We lost some members due to frank talk about money, but that turned out to be a good thing.

Money is a scarce resource, like water hidden underground. It could be tapped under the right conditions, with a dowser's luck.

We have a new minister who is more comfortable talking about money, including giving in good measure as an integral part of membership. An important element was that older members were willing to change their minds about long-established traditions.

The leadership of my church realizes that to solve the money problem would involve taking steps that would make them uncomfortable.

The annual budget is carefully scrutinized. The attitude is how to spend less rather than what we can and should do.

There is an embarrassment in my church about the inability to increase the minister's salary, but there is no initiative on anyone's part to change this culture.

Money contributed to the church becomes a zero-sum game. If one committee gains, another loses.

Money does not enter the spiritual realm, and that is a loss for us.

The church in recent years has found a renewed sense of ministry. Discovering that we can achieve what we set out to do—God's work—has been a real shot in the arm and has improved our stewardship efforts.

In this book, we will determine how churches develop their financial cultures, the length of time current attitudes regarding money have been in place, and the consequences of these cultures, pro and con.

An Entirely Different View

In his compelling book, *Reinventing American Protestantism*, Donald Miller writes:

I believe we are witnessing a second reformation that is transforming the way Christianity will be experienced in the new millennium. The style of Christianity dominated by eighteenth-century hymns, routinized liturgy, and bureaucratized layers of social organization is gradually dying. In its place are emerging hundreds of new paradigm churches, which are appropriating stylistic and organizational elements from our postmodern culture. This reformation, unlike the one led by Martin Luther, is challenging not doctrine but the medium through which the message of Christianity is articulated. But what makes this reformation radical is that the hope of reforming existing denominational churches has largely been abandoned. Instead, the leaders of these new paradigm churches are starting new movements, unbounded by denominational bureaucracy and the restraint of tradition—except the model of first-century Christianity.[2]

Miller also writes, "Many clergy and members of mainline congregations would like to ignore this revolution." However, we cannot overlook the presence of independent churches, because their approach is so radically different, and because some of their methods are superior to mainline faiths. Throughout this book, I'll cite examples of how independent churches vary from the established norm. This is not to suggest that newly formed churches are superior in every regard. All churches have their strengths and weaknesses. Nevertheless, much can be learned from newly formed churches.

The most visible of the new paradigm churches are the megachurches, such as Saddleback Community Church in Southern California, and Willow Creek, just outside Chicago. These churches have memberships of 15,000 people or more. But megachurches are just the tip of the proverbial iceberg. It is estimated that thousands of independent churches have formed in recent decades, and their collective membership numbers in the millions.

A Different View of Money, Also

Clergy and lay leaders of mainline faiths may be surprised to learn that many newly founded churches do not ordinarily experience financial difficulties. Many new churches begin as "house churches," groups of people meeting in homes or apartments, and the founding minister holds a secular job. Overhead expenses are minimal, and the minister does not require a salary. The belief is that if God intends a ministry to grow, it will grow. If not, it won't.

If a house church grows, members at some point will decide they wish the minister to become more involved in the life of the fledgling congregation. Members will make a financial commitment to provide the money for the minister to work either part time or full time on behalf of the church. If the church continues to grow, members will then seek a meeting place outside of a home or apartment.

New churches tend to rent commercial space because they often believe that traditional church architecture and symbols like stained glass windows represent a religion that has failed. Some are "portable" churches that move in and out of places like school auditoria each Sunday. This lessens a church's overhead considerably. If a church does not thrive, the congregation is not stuck with a "religious" structure that may be difficult to unload.

For example, near Boston, a newly formed nondenominational church of 10,000 members meets in a former department store. Whatever the cost of ministry and property, members of new churches make the financial commitment to support the ministry in advance. Surprisingly, there is little talk about money once this commitment has been made. Similar to following other scriptural precepts, giving in generous measure, usually tithing, is an integral part of being a member of a new church.

Some newly formed churches begin in rented properties, then build. Willow Creek and Saddleback Community Church have built spectacular buildings on multiacre sites. These two churches offer seminars and workshops on the subject of church growth that attract thousands of clergy and lay leaders every year. The new church movement has taken to heart author Lyle Schaller's view that "one of the most powerful forces in opposition to the emergence of more very large congregations is the widespread reliance on rule books, both congregational and denominational, that are filled with obsolete, internally inconsistent, and counterproductive rules on how to do church."[3]

The Culture of Money

In mainline churches, an established culture toward money, often decades in the making, can exert a powerful influence on congregational leaders. This can be the case in small and large churches alike, regardless of the amount of money involved. Clergy and lay leaders who make monetary decisions may also have limited experience in finance, accounting, property management, fundraising, or related fields. Sometimes the amount of money managed by volunteers can be significant, involving millions of dollars.

Beyond issues of accounting and finance, clergy, lay leaders, and people in the pews often express highly emotional and conflicting views about how money should be managed and spent. How does the church address competing viewpoints among parishioners? How do clergy and lay leaders develop the expertise and the courage to make good financial decisions—ones that may not make everyone happy, and in fact might anger a segment of the congregation?

Some financial issues may appear simple on the surface, particularly in small churches where dollar amounts are modest. Larger congregations have more complex financial concerns. Churches that own a building (or buildings) have one set of financial issues, while those that rent or lease space have quite another.

The effective management of financial resources is a multifaceted subject in congregations of all ages, sizes, and theologies. Throughout this book, we will examine long-held and perhaps fiercely held views among parishioners about what money should be used for in the first place.

In his perceptive surveys into the habits of American churchgoers, George Barna has come to a distressing conclusion. He writes, "Most pastors, church staff, and lay leaders are both inadequately trained and emotionally unprepared for communicating about and actually raising the kind of money required to lead a church toward the fulfillment of its vision."[4] If Barna is correct, then church leaders require a significant amount of education and assistance in addressing a multitude of issues regarding money and church finance.

This book will identify obstacles that congregations face today. Having identified these challenges, my goal is to offer hope, encouragement, and a wide array of choices that church leaders have available in overcoming these obstacles.

A Cultural Caveat

One of the most important issues we will discuss is whether a congregation's culture can be changed for the better if church leaders don't like what they have now.

This book will help define the culture of churches in regard to money. Culture is sometimes referred to as "how we do things around here," an apt definition. However, clergy and lay leaders should be cautious in thinking that once defined, a congregation's culture can be changed, especially in the short term.

Edgar Schein of the Massachusetts Institute of Technology is a recognized authority on culture in the corporate sector. His views apply to the church world, as well. He writes, "The newspapers are full of managers announcing that they need a 'new culture' of something or other in their organization. . . . Can you imagine saying that the United States, or France, needs a new culture?"[5]

Schein continues by adding, "Unfortunately, many academics and consultants tout culture concepts and theories based on [culture-related] questionnaires that produce numbers and profiles, and that permit organizations to be put into neat boxes. . . . In my experience, the forces that matter cannot be dug out with simple measures; they cannot easily be classified into typologies because they tend to be unique patterns reflecting the unique history of the organization."[6]

In churches, as in corporations, the history, tradition, and established ways of a particular congregation are not subject to simple analysis and quick, turnaround solutions. A congregation's culture is also not monolithic, but consists of many subcultures in various groups and committees. These subcultures may or may not be in alignment, leading the church in a unified direction.

Unfortunately, congregational leaders are often led to believe they can attend a workshop or seminar on various church topics, usually stewardship or church finance, and come away with a prescription that will instantly address the ills the church is facing. We tend to believe that good ideas presented at seminars will be embraced by the congregation back home. This is not necessarily the case, because of the long-established culture of church communities.

The All Important Vision

Congregational leaders are also led to believe that if they clarify the mission or vision of the church, parishioners will give more money. Churches should have clear missions and visions, but in my experience, many statements are lengthy, vague, and ambiguous, and are not internalized by the minister or the congregation. For example, can you recite the mission of your own church? Many churchgoers cannot.

Churches formulate their missions in different ways. In mainline churches, various groups or committees are often set to the task of formulating the mission. This is usually followed by a series of discussions involving church members, and a congregational vote is sometimes required for approval.

In newly formed churches, the minister is often the founder and is solely responsible for setting a clear mission. People who join subscribe to that mission and work toward its accomplishment. The mission is not formulated by means of a congregational vote.

Whatever the church, congregations with established patterns of low-level and same-level giving will not suddenly become generous because the mission statement is rewritten. Only through living out its mission and realizing its vision will a church become a community whose members grow in faith, hope, and charity.

In my experience, mainline denominations have begun to take some cues from high-expectation churches. For example, when a new mainline church is planted, the founding members are often called to considerably higher standards of giving and service than in long-established parishes. They may not applaud wildly when the offering is announced at the Sunday service, as is the custom in some new churches,[7] but these founding members realize that a significant commitment is required to establish and maintain a new church.

Looking Forward or Letting Go?

Professor Schein has also observed that, "A change in culture often involves unlearning, letting go of things that may be valued by many."[8] I frequently encounter this aspect of church life. For many people, church is one of the most stable and predictable elements in their lives. Parishioners derive great meaning from the ritual and tradition of church.

In many mainline churches, prayer books and hymnals that were printed long ago accompany rituals of worship. Thus, parishioners do not expect to come to church and find things changed around. They prefer the familiar.

Newly formed churches take a dramatically different view. One significant difference is that new churches are nontraditional to begin with. They start with a clean slate, and they do not inherit denominational customs. In most new churches, a set of core beliefs is nonnegotiable, and parishioners seem to be more willing to accept changes in worship and how the church conducts its various ministries as long as these core beliefs remain intact.

For example, new churches were among the first to initiate four or five different worship services each weekend—including rock and roll services and worship that feature contemporary Christian music, dance, video, and congregations that don't sit still but express joy and exuberance during worship. The emphasis in new churches is not on "The Word" as in traditional faiths, but on "The Experience" of a living God.

Although writing about secular corporations, Schein illumines key aspects of established church life. He writes, "Members of a group want to hold on to their cultural assumptions because culture provides meaning and makes life predictable. Humans do not like chaotic, unpredictable situations and work hard to stabilize and 'normalize' them. Any prospective culture change therefore launches massive amounts of anxiety and resistance to change."[9]

In my work with mainline congregations, I encourage church leaders to focus not only on the church's mission and what lies ahead, but also on the shared values the congregation has held for many years. In particular, we discuss whether these deeply held assumptions serve primarily those who are currently in church, and make it difficult for newcomers to become part of the community. These assumptions include the most honored and ingrained elements of church life, including the time of worship, the order of service, type of music, and various rituals.

The rituals and customs that congregations find most familiar may be the most daunting to newcomers. How often do we see visitors struggling to find their place in a hymnal or prayer book, while the rest of the congregation has commenced singing or reading? This can be embarrassing to visitors, as it portrays them as out of step. Traditional faiths assume a high level of familiarity on the part of those attending church.

In contrast, worship services of new paradigm churches are almost always geared toward people who are there for the first time. These churches attempt to lessen the distance between unchurched souls and their experience with the Divine.

Thus, in mainline faiths, the voice of God may not be calling established congregations to move toward the future as much as to loosen their grasp on the past. This doesn't mean that parishioners who sit quietly and listen to Bach should welcome rock and roll musicians, or stand and wave their arms during worship. However, I do believe congregations can adapt to changing times without compromising their integrity and tradition.

Not Entirely Logical

Because of their volunteer nature, churches are often inconsistent in how they are managed and administered. Some churches might be viewed as defying logic. This can be alternately endearing and frustrating to church leaders and parishioners alike. On paper, it might be demonstrated that some churches should have closed long ago, yet they display a tenacity for life that many believe indicates the presence of God.

However, we cannot overlook the disheartening comments from clergy and lay leaders summarized earlier in this chapter. Unfortunately, recurring financial problems are daily fare for the leaders of many traditional churches. In the United States today, 85 percent of mainline churches are estimated to be on a plateau in membership or in decline. Established churches today face increasingly complex issues that will require ever-greater skill, expertise, and flexibility on the part of decision makers. Unfortunately, congregational leaders all too often find themselves faced with outdated ideas, ineffective policies, and institutionalized bad habits that are entrenched in the life of the church.

The wise and effective use of money at church is not just a matter of finance or administration. It is a central issue for an increasing number of churches to stay alive. Congregational leaders need to acquire the knowledge and confidence to steer their churches in an environment that is increasingly indifferent and sometimes hostile to religious expression.

Guiding a church in these times is a journey that presents significant challenges. When people come to church, they wish to be in the presence of God. They want to get along with their fellow parishioners. They don't want to get into disagreements with their friends and neighbors. They desire a "higher order" of things. In turn, congregational leaders hope they will make decisions that guide the church toward the realm of the Holy.

While churches are instruments of God's work, they are also human institutions, subject to the widest range of human failings. A church, in fact, may be the ultimate volunteer organization. As such, the well-being of parishioners may be more important than how business is conducted. This book addresses the subject of money, but church finance is based on a wide range of issues regarding congregational life that confront, confound, delight, and frustrate clergy and lay leaders.

In order for churches to chart a course for the future, we need to determine the extent to which religion is a factor in the lives of people in the first place. This is the subject of the next chapter.

CHAPTER TWO

Whatever Happened to Sunday?

Today, in the United States, the norm, even among churchgoing Christians, is a secularized family, with very little religious practice actually going on in the home.

Rosemary Radford Reuther[1]

Creating vital and engaging congregations is the main focus of this book. Our success in doing this, however, is determined in large part by the value of religion in the hearts, minds, and souls of churchgoers today. People are unlikely to invest their time or money in a church (or any endeavor) that does not engage them at some fundamental level. Unfortunately, the real or perceived value of church has diminished significantly for millions of people.

An important aspect of church involvement is attendance at worship, traditionally on Sunday morning. For many families, however, Sunday morning now involves participating in a sports league for children or adults, eating breakfast at a restaurant, going to the grocery store, gardening, doing office work that has been brought home, or engaging in other nonchurch activities. Sunday morning might also mean sleeping in, the only downtime for adults who lead hectic lives and for "overprogrammed" children. The concept of the Sabbath, a day set aside for sacred pursuits, may strike many as a quaint anachronism.

The secular, consumer-oriented society of the United States has had a profound effect on how Americans view religious practice and whether they participate in a community of faith at all. Churches today face a withering array of challenges in restoring and maintaining their value—even to those who attend church. In a letter to the Alban Institute's *Congregations* magazine, Presbyterian minister Daniel Wolpert wrote:

> In order for pastors to be spiritual leaders, the members of the congregation have to be spiritual seekers, and this is not something that can be said about most American Christians. . . . Only a tiny percentage of the lay people in the church are actually interested in spiritual growth. The vast majority are there . . . out of a sense of obligation or habit, or to socialize, or to make a good showing among their peer group. Thus, the majority of the people who I am supposed to lead . . . couldn't care less about how Jesus might change their lives.[2]

If Wolpert is correct that only a small proportion of *people who go to church* are seeking spiritual lives, then the message that charitable giving is a meaningful aspect of faith development and the religious life has a very small audience.

Churchgoers aside, how is the religious life viewed by millions of people who do not attend church? Large numbers of people have no interest in church whatsoever. In his surveys, George Barna has concluded, "When you scrape away all the excuses and niceties, most nonchurched people avoid church involvement because they fail to see any compelling reason to invest the time and energy. . . . [They believe] that churches have nothing of real benefit to offer."[3]

At the same time, countless nonchurched people seek spirituality through a booming business in spiritually oriented books, videotapes, retreats, lectures, and courses. These people seem to believe they will not find a spiritual life within organized religion. They tend to seek spirituality, a type of inner peace, but not religion as manifested in the institution of the church.

Barna's surveys also reveal that people believe "spiritual enlightenment comes from diligence in a discovery process, rather than commitment to a faith group and perspective," and they view "religion as a commodity that we consume, rather than one in which we invest ourselves."[4]

A Golden Age Gone By?

In decades past, much of life in America revolved around three major elements: work, family, and church. Today, churches face ever-increasing competition from television, movies, professional sports, and a multitude of other secular activities. The repeal of blue laws has turned Sunday into just another shopping day, with even liquor stores open in various locales.

In my own community, I walk past a restaurant and a bagel shop on the way to church. On Sunday mornings these places are filled with parents in sweat clothes, with tousled hair, drinking coffee and skimming the newspapers, their children in tow, barely out of pajamas. These rumpled families stand in stark contrast to people who are going to or coming from church. Somewhere along the line it became acceptable to appear disheveled in public on Sunday morning, though it is less acceptable any other time of the week. We are at a far remove from the Puritan days of New England, when a person could be arrested by the civil authorities for not being in church on Sunday.

I often ask people if they received a certificate or a pin for perfect attendance at Sunday school when they were children. A surprising number have. Many people still have these pins among their keepsakes. When I ask clergy and lay leaders if their churches maintain the tradition of perfect attendance awards, most say they do not. Many congregations cannot envision perfect attendance, the only exception being the pastor's family. In many communities, Sunday morning soccer wins out.

An important question that church leaders should pose to congregants is whether Sunday morning sports or other activities are more important than being together at church. One soccer mom, a board member in her church, told me she finds love, warmth, and fellowship among parents at Sunday morning games that she does not find at worship. She wished it were otherwise. She yearned for a deeper faith, one that addressed the ultimate meaning of life, but did not find this at church. She was reluctant to share her feelings with the minister or with fellow congregants.

High-expectation faiths such as the Church of Jesus Christ of Latter-day Saints (Mormons) prohibit members from engaging in organized sports and commercial activities on Sunday. For churchgoing families of less demanding faiths, the choice is not as clear-cut.

Fierce Competition

I succumbed to Sunday morning sports myself. For ten consecutive Sundays I did not attend worship services at my church. Instead, I stood on the sidelines and watched my twelve-year-old son play Pop Warner football. Those who believe I should have "just said no" to my child's request should know that from a young age my son disliked church. My father was forced to go to church when he was a child, and he never went back again. I conceded football for a few months because I didn't want this to happen to my son.

The most startling surprise of having a child on the team was the commitment of time, effort, and money required of parents. As one who has recruited Sunday school teachers and committee members over the years, I am all too familiar with excuses people give for not having the time. The overcommitted parent, however, does not exist in Pop Warner football. Or more accurately, parents have little choice. They participate and follow the rules, or their children do not play.

Football players as young as eight years of age practice three times each week, rain or shine, and a parent is expected to be at all practices. Games are on Sunday, and "away" games are played at towns up to sixty miles distant. Parents often leave home at 7:00 or 8:00 on Sunday mornings, and do not return until 1:00 or 2:00 P.M.

Few churches would dare ask for this commitment of parishioners! Yet football parents do not question it. They believe the benefits to their children are worth it. What are these benefits? Teamwork? Sportsmanship? The thrill of winning? A trophy? An eventual athletic scholarship? What might churches claim as benefits that rival Sunday morning football, soccer, or other activities?

Pop Warner football is not "boys only." Each team also has a complement of same-age girls as cheerleaders, so parents of young girls have an equal commitment of practice, schedules, and games. The cost of uniforms and equipment is extra, and parents are expected to raise money for the league. Some raise as much as $500 in a few weeks, an amount greater than the median pledge in my church. Parents also sell raffle tickets, T-shirts and hats, staff the refreshment booth, and hold marker chains along the sidelines. Much of this work is done outdoors in the rain, cold, wind, and snow. Were it so easy for churches to receive this commitment from parents and families!

Is it possible for the contemporary family to find time for church and youth sports? Now that Sunday morning sports leagues are well established, will children be resentful about going to church when their friends are on the playing field? Churchgoing families need help and support to reach a resolution.

The Massachusetts Council of Churches encourages religious people to speak out against youth sports on Sunday morning. The Council also notes with alarm the increasing number of walks, bicycle races, and other special events that are scheduled on Sunday. One example was a parade that ended on a church lawn, with loudspeakers blaring while members of the church were inside during worship.

"Because many of these events are for charitable purposes," the Council writes, "it heightens the dilemma for community-minded churchgoers. But the larger issue is a pattern of public insensitivity to the religious traditions of our churches." The Council has assembled a packet of materials for clergy and lay leaders on how to negotiate with community residents who schedule Sunday events.[5]

Not Just Sports

One of the most egregious examples of public insensitivity to religious tradition and worship is the inclusion of African American churches as tour destinations. Columnist and law professor Patricia Williams writes:

> In black neighborhoods around the United States, but most particularly in well-known communities like Harlem in New York, busloads of tourists flock to black churches on Sunday morning, or any other time for that matter, gate-crashing baptisms and choir rehearsals, prayer groups and funerals. . . . Caravans of Swedes and Japanese and Dutch and Brazilians fight with congregants for good seats, straining for the perfect camera angles, hunkering down for a good show. It's great theater, according to the guidebook list of hits, all those black people dressed in their quaint finery, singing and swooning and singing some more.[6]

Voyeurism of religious practice is certainly not new. In the nineteenth century, it was common for nonbelievers to attend worship services of The Second Coming of Believers in Christ (the Shakers), and view the rituals of dancing and shaking. Guests, however, were expected to sit quietly and respect the custom and traditions of the worshipers.

Today, however, even church members take flash photographs or operate video cameras during worship when their children sing in the choir or have a role in the service. Worship is viewed as a performance, not unlike a school play or piano recital. As worship is diminished, so is our ability to find the sacred in liturgy.

Congregants of many faiths have also been reeling from a staggering array of banner headlines about clergy misconduct, embezzlement of church funds, sexual abuse of children, and liberal vs. conservative arguments that portray both sides as rigid and unyielding. It may be increasingly difficult even for dedicated Christians to maintain their belief in the institutions of faith, given the widespread media coverage of these disheartening events.

If People Do Come to Church

The Right Reverend Charles Bennison, Episcopal Bishop of Pennsylvania, has written a wonderful account about people in church:

> On Sunday mornings, people leave behind the circles they frequent and the routines they follow, and they come. They come mad, they come glad, and they come sad. They come eagerly, they come automatically, they come deliberately, they come expectantly, and they come reluctantly. Some come thinking that nothing really will happen, and others come hoping everything will happen. Some come bored and contemptuous by the familiarity of it all, and others come frightened by its unfamiliarity. Some come out of loyalty to their religious backgrounds, and others come in rebellion against their backgrounds. Some come with an easy sense of self-satisfaction, and others come with a guilty sense of dissatisfaction. They are a mixed group of saints and sinners, sheep and goats, wheat and tares, what Luther called a *corpus mixtum*. Still, for all these reasons, they come.[7]

Or, for these reasons, they do not come. In many established churches, less than half the members attend Sunday worship services.

Conflicting attitudes toward church are not limited to laypersons alone. In his book, *A New Kind of Christian*, the Reverend Brian McLaren addresses his disillusionment in a powerful story about his own loss of faith. He writes:

> I wrote in my journal that one year from today, I would no longer be in the ministry. But I had not yet discovered that I could become a Christian in a new way. What if God was actually behind this disillusionment? Shouldn't the gospel of Jesus Christ make a bigger difference? Doesn't the

religious community see that the world is changing? Doesn't it have anything fresh and incisive to say? As I shared my feelings with others, I found many people who believed likewise.[8]

A Meaning in Faith

The Reverend Victor Carpenter, my minister and close friend, often claimed that "small miracles occur in church every Sunday." I believe he is right. Millions of people attend Sunday worship because it is an integral part of their lives. But for as many people who find special meaning in worship, there are as many who do not.

People come to church because they want to, and because they find something of value there. I don't expect people will consider charitable giving (in any measure) until they discern some tangible religious meaning. Can you write down on a piece of paper what your church offers you that is of significant value? What do you and your fellow parishioners find of meaning, in which you invest your time, effort, and money—willingly and joyfully?

I believe the stewardship conversation begins here, with an engaging message that proclaims what church is all about and why people should be involved. Jesus was bold in his ministry. His message was very clear. Churches should act likewise.

All too often, unfortunately, mainline churches are hesitant to define what the church stands for, the expectations of membership, and what it means to be part of an authentic community of faith. The membership literature of churches often contains noncommittal and lukewarm phrases such as, "You may not be a joiner," "You don't need to become a member," "You don't need to make a commitment," and "You can join whenever you get around to it." This can result in a "Church of the Uncommitted," a phrase used by a board chair to describe his church.

In contrast, another lay leader in a seminar once spoke about "integrity of membership" in her church, and what that meant. This led to a compelling discussion in which we eventually came around to the following description of membership:

At times, churches are places of comfort, respite, and solace. But not always. Sometimes churches present great challenges. Sometimes we may be asked to give small amounts of time, effort, or money. But sometimes the church might ask us to make the most significant commitment we've made in our entire lives. And sometimes we may be asked to make the largest charitable gift we've ever made. This is the nature of churches. Anyone coming into this church should know what's in store—perhaps a roller-coaster ride, perhaps one of the greatest adventures of a lifetime.

Membership, Continued

I also find churches reluctant to ask parishioners to do much, yet concerned that a small number of people carry the workload. Many mainline churches are also extremely tentative about the expectations of charitable giving, instead of displaying the wonderful array of benefits that derive from being a generous person or family.

In contrast, newly formed churches are not hesitant whatsoever to articulate the meaning of church. This includes reaching out to others and heeding the Great Commission (Matthew 28:19). These churches rely on what is called "first-century communication." Jesus and his disciples did not have telephones, fax machines, or e-mail. The disciples communicated with one another face-to-face about the faith that had changed their lives so dramatically.

People wish to be a meaningful part of meaningful organizations, and church-seekers are often described as people who are on self-identified religious pilgrimages. Many established churches, alas, do not assist people in making these journeys of faith. Churches all too often leave newcomers on their own to figure out what the church is all about. A church leader once said to me, "If visitors have questions, they can ask for answers." Visitors may not ask questions. They are more likely to seek churches that willingly and effectively share the good news.

Newly formed churches leave no doubt what they stand for. New churches have not varied the theology as much as the medium in which it is presented. New churches tend to believe that a certain amount of "strictness" provides members with a more thorough explanation of life.[9] In a fractious world, these churches offer "something that is unchanging, eternal, and divinely inspired."[10] Absent in many of these churches is "fundamentalism's vehement opposition to modernity."[11] New churches have adapted to the times. Many are culturally avant-garde.

I believe clergy, lay leaders, and people in the pews in traditional churches have let the spirit of religion and evangelism fade away. I include myself in this group. Many Christians are reluctant to discuss their faith with others, and the church provides little support in teaching parishioners how to do this well. This is not the strident evangelism that members of mainline faiths find so distasteful, but rather a heartfelt sharing with others about what faith means to us. A vast difference separates the two. Unfortunately, many of us keep our faith private.

One of the saddest conclusions that George Barna's surveys have brought to light is the response when people are asked, "How many people do you encounter who reflect a 'Christian' lifestyle, values system, or countenance?" Barna reports that "most adults claim they know of very few people, if any, whose lives are clearly transformed or consistently guided by their religious faith."[12]

I believe a key to reviving mainline congregations is for churchgoers to share the value of their religious lives with others. I urge readers to express their views more openly about what they find in church that cannot be found in secular life. We should all share more willingly the reasons we go to church, how our lives are enriched, why we work on its behalf, and why we support the church financially in ample measure.

I believe that discipleship and effective stewardship go hand in hand. We are called to create churches that reach out and serve. This is a far cry from asking people for money to pay the church's bills. Until people of faith are willing to become bolder in this adventure called religion, I believe large numbers of traditional, mainline churches will be perceived by the public (and possibly by churchgoers and their ministers alike!) as increasingly weak and possibly irrelevant. Churches like this are not places where people put their hearts, their souls, or their treasures. The Great Commission goes unheeded, not only for us, but for generations to come. And we are all the less because of it.

CHAPTER THREE

Brother, Can You Spare a Dime?

I work in one of the wealthiest areas in the country, but churches here struggle with a starvation mentality.

The Reverend Anne Johnson, United Church of Christ

A pervasive attitude of scarcity ranks high among the most debilitating aspects of mainline churches today. This attitude is present even in affluent congregations. The perception of scarcity cuts across most denominational and geographic boundaries.

A major cause of scarcity in mainline churches derives from a widely followed, commonplace practice. That practice is asking parishioners to support the operating budget of the church through the annual pledge drive. The operating budget, with its familiar line items, is usually the centerpiece. Clergy and staff are to be paid. The building requires heat, light, and insurance. Committees need to know how much they can spend. The Sunday school needs snacks. In sum, the church's bills are ever present.

Many churches also approve a "tight" budget for the coming fiscal year, which means that costs must be kept in check. A church treasurer recently told me, "A tight budget has become a stranglehold on the affairs of this church, fiscal and otherwise—a constant reminder of why we can't do things around here."

As important as each line item may be, the operating budget is not an inspiration for giving. Charitable giving is an expression of faith and the religious life, not paying the church's bills. The basis for true stewardship is the meaning and joy that people derive from sharing in adequate measure. Being a generous person or family is one of life's great privileges—one of the hallmarks of a life well lived.

This concept of stewardship is often found in conservative, newly founded, and high expectation churches. These churches create congregations of generous people, ironically, by rarely talking about money. Becoming a person of faith is based on Scripture, and sharing in ample measure is viewed as little different from other precepts that call us to lead godly lives. In many new churches, an annual financial statement is distributed at the end of the year, but the budget is rarely visible and has little to do with charitable giving.

Unfortunately, in traditional churches, the message of heartfelt giving is often overshadowed by an emphasis on the operating budget. Viewed line by line, the operating budget may inadvertently create antipathy toward giving. Things at church tend to cost more each year, and the budget can become the focus of considerable debate about why certain items cost so much, and is it possible to get by on less?

The tradition of carefully scrutinizing the budget usually occurs at a church's annual meeting. Much energy can be focused on particular line items rather than on charitable giving as an integral aspect of religious life. I recall a congregant standing up at an annual meeting and braying loudly, "I see the membership committee has requested $50 more this year. Can someone tell me what they plan to do with this money?"

A culture of scarcity in traditional churches can be decades in the making. This culture may be particularly discouraging to the generous souls who contribute the most (usually one-third of congregants contribute about 75 percent of the church's annual income, and about the same percentage of capital campaigns). These church pillars love the church and often labor mightily on its behalf. These dedicated souls usually do not raise stewardship issues at annual meetings, but I believe they should! The least generous voices often go unchallenged and too frequently prevail. It is rare for someone to stand up and recommend the congregation pay *more* for something, even if this is the wisest course.

Churches founded in recent decades have not carried forward this tradition. Newly formed congregations embody two approaches we will explore throughout the book. The first includes churches that "front-end" expectations of membership and giving. Newcomers know full well what the expectations are, and in some churches are not permitted to join until they make this recognized commitment. In other churches, one's involvement and level of giving are expected to grow as a person's faith or spiritual life develops more fully. Neither approach to charitable giving includes the operating budget.

How Money Plays Out in Local Parishes

Sometimes money is in short supply, but sometimes it is only perceived to be. Whether a financial shortcoming is real or imaginary, church leaders can find themselves swept up in excessive oversight of the operating budget, scrutinizing expenses and scrimping wherever possible. This can reach absurd proportions. I recall a 700-member church issuing a call in its newsletter for donations of scrap paper for the church office. A physician responded with a gargantuan quantity of memo pads from a pharmaceutical company, and for months thereafter the church's informal business was conducted on paper that carried an advertisement for an antipsychotic drug.

Lyle Schaller is one of the most articulate voices in American religious studies. His belief is that "the most common source of passivity in a congregation is the effect of the sense of mission's being eroded and replaced by a priority on institutional self-preservation. Many of the members intuitively feel this is incompatible with the basic nature of a Christian congregation, and they begin to lose interest."[1] If a church expends it credibility on appeals for scrap paper, it will dilute its call for people to lead lives of stronger faith.

I hasten to add that newcomers are wary of a church that displays anxiety toward money. They fear they will be asked to bail the church out of financial problems that are not of their making. Congregational leaders should avoid heightening tension around finances, especially in churches with ample reserves.

Only in Church?

The widespread attitude of scarcity has created a concept that I call "the three leasts." Congregational leaders often wish to know the least amount of time, the least amount of effort, and the least amount of money required to address stewardship or financial issues.

This concept of "The three leasts" applies in even the most affluent congregations. I recently received a telephone call from a church in an affluent community. This church has no debt, $1.5 million in accumulated funds, and assets of $3 million. The church had experienced a $20,000 shortfall in revenue in the operating budget, and the leadership was talking about cutting back on programs and activities.

When I visited this church, the minister and lay leaders displayed a palpable anxiety about money. This attitude had permeated throughout the congregation. The minister had spoken about the "fiscal crisis" from the pulpit a number of times. Some parishioners wondered if hiring a half-time youth minister the year before had been a mistake now that money was tight. Some offered a glimmer of hope that new members coming in might help pay the church's bills. What was the church to do? The twelve-member board could have easily pledged the additional $20,000, but they were unwilling to do so. They were also unwilling to ask the congregation to make up the shortfall. They wondered if I had any great ideas about where to find money—fast!

The culture of "leasts" is often present in churches but usually not in our private lives. When contemplating an item we wish to purchase, a familiar refrain is, "Well, it costs a little more, but you get what you pay for." If parents are seeking a music teacher for their children, the first thought is usually not, "Let's find the cheapest." If we are ill, we do not usually contemplate which doctor charges the least, but seek appropriate medical care. We tend to seek the best for ourselves and our families, not the cheapest.

My experience is that churches spend money prudently, and financial decisions are made with great thought and care. This is a good thing. However, churches also tend to create a "rummage sale" mentality, always looking for a bargain.

Occasionally parishioners supplement their contributions with cast-off items that are no longer useful in their own homes. The radio commentator Paul Harvey once told a story about a woman who called the Butterball Turkey company. She found a turkey that had been in the freezer for twenty-three years, and she asked whether it was any good. She was told that if the freezer was at least zero degrees during that time, the turkey was probably still safe enough to eat, but they wouldn't recommend it because the flavor would have deteriorated considerably. She replied, "That's what I thought. I guess I'll just give it to the church."

Not the Only Culprit

Let's take a look at two other common issues surrounding money in the traditional church. These all-too-frequent attitudes will help determine how anxiety around money is created in the first place, then perpetuated in thousands of churches across the land.

Poor Habit #1: We don't talk about money.

Ministers are accustomed to people revealing extraordinarily intimate details of their lives. These include family tragedies, alcoholism, sexual abuse, and all manner of dysfunctional behavior. Yet a person's financial situation is off-limits, far too personal to share. We keep our financial affairs private.

Silence around money is a powerful taboo that weakens vitality in traditional churches. Robert Wood Lynn, a consultant and historian, has referred to this silence as a "conspiratorial secrecy."

A great deal of secrecy around money stems from our perceptions of how much money other people may or may not have. Parishioners who display outward signs of wealth must have plenty of money, so it is easy for them to be charitable. For others, to raise the issue of money can create numerous anxieties. We may not have much money, and others might find out. We may have managed our money poorly or gotten into debt. We may wish to maintain secrecy about our own level of giving. If the subject of money comes up at church, we may be asked to give more, an unpleasant thought for many. Plus, nobody likes asking other people for money, anyway. If we can avoid these unpleasant conversations, so much the better. All this leads to the next poor habit.

Poor Habit #2: Nobody has much money, anyway.

My church is located in an affluent community (Median Family Income over $100,000), and I led the annual pledge drive during the

1990s, the most prosperous decade in American history. When I spoke about sharing in greater measure, numerous people said to me gravely, "These are hard times, and people are struggling. This is not a good time to ask for more."

This reminded me of an anecdote from a delightful book by Ashley Hale titled *The Lost Art of Church Fundraising*. He writes, "When I was Operations Manager of the largest church fund raising management company, I sought the best time to raise funds. An exhaustive study came in with a clear answer. There is no best time to raise funds. They are all bad."[2]

The 1990s brought staggering increases in the sales of luxury cars, trophy homes, designer clothes, plastic surgery, lottery tickets, and a plethora of expensive and unnecessary items like cashmere sweaters for dogs. Extravagant weddings costing tens of thousands of dollars are back in style. Numerous communities have instituted "anti-mansion" laws, attempting to stop the proliferation of grossly oversized houses.

This era also brought us "personal shoppers," so that we are assured of acquiring items of good taste. If we buy too much, we can engage a "clutter consultant" at a high hourly rate to help organize our overstuffed closets. (The National Association of Professional Organizers now boasts a membership of over 1,500 people.)

While ostentatious spending may not reflect the habits of the typical churchgoer, more middle-class and working-class parishioners than ever before lead comfortable, well-appointed lives. However, their behavior tends to resemble that of paupers upon passing through the church's doors.

In their book *The State of Church Giving through 1997*, noted researchers John and Sylvia Ronsvalle summarize charitable giving to churches from 1968 to 1997. Their data reveal that giving to churches increased during this period, but decreased as a percentage of income. In other words, as we earned more, we gave less. Per capita giving in 1997, near the end of the most prosperous decade in United States history, was lower than it was in 1933, during the Great Depression.[3]

Not All Boats Rose in the Water

Admittedly, the prosperity of the 1990s did not reach all American families. Numerous studies indicate that many families did not benefit

48

from the economic gains of the most prosperous era in American history.

I believe churches need to assess local economic conditions in the geographical areas in which their churches are located. What percent of the congregation is doing well financially, gaining in income and assets? What percentage may be just holding its own? What percentage is losing ground? And what percentage may be slipping into or actually living in poverty, without health insurance and other basic needs?

This book is for middle-class and working-class churches, the mainstream of American religion. While churchgoers can experience financial hardships, they do not live in poverty. They have discretionary income. Economists who study the financial habits of American citizens indicate that most people could double their charitable giving and not notice the difference in their daily lives.

Today, professional sports events, concerts, and other entertainment venues attract millions of middle-class and blue-collar fans. Ticket prices have increased exponentially, some now in the hundreds of dollars. The price of concessions at these events has also skyrocketed. A family of four attending a Major League Baseball game can expect to spend as much as $150 to $200, given the cost of tickets, parking, and refreshments.

A minister who serves a church in New England said it is common for families to spend $1,500 for a ski weekend or twice that much for a trip to Disney World, while believing that $250 or $500 is an adequate pledge to the church. The high cost of entertainment is now acceptable to millions of middle-class and working-class Americans. Yet the culture in many churches is the widespread belief that people are struggling financially and that large portions of the congregation cannot possibly give more than they currently do—even if giving is low and no one knows what other people give.

In the 1990s, overt greed and ostentation was often portrayed in the media as "the good life." Is this the legacy we will leave our children and grandchildren? Is not gross excess, or conversely, extreme miserliness, the antithesis of a religious life?

Princeton University Professor Robert Wuthnow, director of the Center for the Study of American Religion, addresses this issue in his book *The Crisis in the Churches: Spiritual Malaise, Fiscal Woe.* In three chapters on stewardship and charitable giving, he suggests that we may decry the gross materialism of the times, but this does not diminish our desire to lead the good life ourselves.[4]

This book is about money in church, but the real issue is how we lead our lives. Charles Spencer of the Presbyterian Church (USA) believes the most powerful stewardship message of our time is the slogan, "There are some things in life that money can't buy—but for everything else there is MasterCard." The good life, indeed, is within easy reach with that small rectangle of plastic. Surely, the religious life involves more than increasingly frequent trips to the mall.

Yet with Americans in dogged pursuit of the material life, anxiety about money is extraordinarily high. A theologian by the single name of Thandeka has coined the phrase "middle-class poverty" to describe people who spend inappropriately to maintain appearances. She writes:

> Many middle-class Americans are pretending to be what they are not: well off. They live in houses they cannot afford, drive cars they do not own, and wear clothes they've bought on credit. Worse yet, toward the end of each pay period, they use their credit cards to buy food. My term for this is middle-class poverty. This late 20th century phenomenon has crippled the American soul.[5]

My colleague Robert Bacon once noted that hidden in the discussion about people's money is that large numbers of people who are wealthy by any objective standard do not perceive themselves so. It used to be that "keeping up with the Joneses" meant the average American family viewed their immediate neighbors as economic peers. Thus, when the proverbial Joneses got a new kitchen appliance, other neighbors followed suit. Now, with the barrage of media attention devoted to upscale homes, expensive cars, exotic vacations, and all the other expressions of the good life, even people who are comfortable financially feel they are down the economic scale because they compare themselves with the wealthy Jones family that is no longer an economic peer.

We may believe that stewardship begins with the mission of the church, but decisions about charitable giving for many families are made long before they set foot in the building—by the way they spend money in their day-to-day lives. The siren song of the American advertising industry is far more melodic than the stewardship message of the church.

The spending habits of Americans now involve issues of both economics and justice. It is estimated that the average American household carries between $6,000 and $7,000 in credit card debt. With interest rates of 18 percent or more, that average household pays between $1,080 and $1,260 in interest each year. American families may be paying hundreds of millions of dollars in interest charges each year for consumer items that were used up long ago. Surely there is a better use for this huge amount of money.

Most traditional churches do not expect parishioners to reduce their standard of living to increase charitable giving. The Assembly of God church, however, encourages its members to live in less expensive homes, drive less expensive cars, and live a more modest lifestyle so they can give more to God. I believe churches of all faiths should challenge the material life in relation to what it means to be a person of faith. Should not churches act as partners in helping parishioners shape lives of dignity, worth, and meaning by how they live day to day? We live in a society in which a person's value is increasingly measured by income, clothes, size of house, and choice of automobile. I believe churches should combat this "you are what you can buy" mentality by providing alternatives to the ever-greater acquisition of consumer goods, and ever-greater acquisition of consumer debt.

The questions I bring to congregations in my work are, "What amount of material goods do we truly need? Beyond that, what luxuries might we provide ourselves? Beyond these luxuries, what extravagances might we also give ourselves? But once we've provided for ourselves in more than ample measure, what are our obligations to share what God has provided?"

Our spending habits should reflect our religious values. George Kinder articulates this concept in his observation that "a sharp divide separates money and soul."[6] He also writes of a chasm between our economic lives and our meditative lives. This chasm is where the work of the church lies.

If I were to single out one issue that is the most important in this book, one issue that I would "charge" clergy and lay leaders to address, it would be the observation made by James Hudnut-Beumler. He writes, "The church must be the institution that validates our nonmaterial values. We may believe that wealth will not make us happy, but not knowing how to be happy otherwise, we strive to become rich."[7] I believe the church falls woefully short regarding this critical aspect of money in contemporary life.

Creating a Giving Church Where One Does Not Currently Exist

Clergy and lay leaders in traditional churches who wish to approach stewardship in a more creative manner need a starting point. It bears repeating that this starting point is to determine parishioners' attitudes toward a number of basic issues regarding congregational life. What do parishioners find of value at the church? Why do they invest in this community of faith?

Self-reflection is also required. Do church leaders themselves find fulfillment, meaning, reward, or joy in charitable giving? Are they willing to make a sacrifice for their faith? Do they communicate this to the congregation? Are people encouraged to share in good measure as an integral aspect of religious life? Does the church use its financial resources for the greater good, or does it save money in endowments or rainy day funds that allow current members to give a pittance? Does the church have a "can do" attitude toward starting new ministries in God's name—or is the refrain all too often, "We don't have the money to do that."

Without knowing the congregation's attitudes toward these issues, church leaders will be relegated to the tedious task of asking parishioners each year for money to support the operating budget. By assessing parishioners' attitudes toward money in their daily lives, church leaders can create a climate within the congregation that encourages open dialogue and counters the pervasive attitudes of secrecy, silence, and scarcity.

Begin at the Beginning

A key factor in creating a congregation of generous people is clarifying the expectations of membership and giving for newcomers. In my work with congregations of traditional faiths, this is the weakest aspect of church life. My view is that many people find great meaning in tithing (giving 10 percent of their income) and that all should be encouraged to do so. Not all will respond, of course, but an ever-growing number of generous souls is a wonderful sight to behold. A congregation like this will attract brave and adventuresome souls.

Until the deeper and more heartfelt issue of sharing in good measure is clarified, articulated, and discussed among congregants, stewardship will remain a predictable event at best. How much will people give? Probably about the same as last year. As older, higher-level donors pass away, they are unlikely to be replaced by younger, lower-level donors. This is the bleak reality for many traditional churches.

Stewardship is not asking people for money. Stewardship is an engaging and ongoing conversation about lives of faith and meaning. Giving is the nature of God, and congregations should reflect God's nature by providing many opportunities for people to give of themselves—throughout the church year and throughout their lives. The next chapter offers some practical steps in doing just that.

CHAPTER FOUR

Making the Annual Pledge Drive Obsolete

The annual pledge drive in my church is a kind of congregational root canal.

Jeff Bradley, pledge drive volunteer

In mainline churches, inordinate amounts of time, effort, and angst go into the pledge drive each year—with the result, as noted, that most people give about the same as the year before.

It bears repeating that the key to making the annual pledge drive obsolete is abandoning the practice of asking parishioners for money. People in the pews often feel harangued to give more each year just to keep pace with inflation and other costs. Pledge drive volunteers can also find the job unrewarding. My father made household visits for his church, and a parishioner once remarked, "You know what I've noticed about the church? It's always broke!"

Entrenched giving can become the norm, and traditional pledge drives based on the operating budget may inadvertently create congregations of grudging donors. Each year, the search continues for increasingly clever (some would say manipulative) ways to ask people for more money. In response, the attitude among parishioners sometimes is, "Okay, convince me to give more, and this better be good." If the pledge drive falls short, members of the stewardship committee may blame themselves for not coming up with an effective approach.

A new theme each year is a common practice, resulting in a plethora of fund-raising schemes and ploys. These include dinners, skits, witty songs, poems, and a host of ways to convince and cajole people into giving to the church. While such events gather people together and are fun, the focus is on fund-raising and not the larger and more significant issues on which charitable giving is based.

The bishop of the Mormon Church in my community once asked me, "Why do you have to convince people over and over, year after year, to support the church? Why don't they just do what they know they are supposed to do?" A good question, indeed, and one we will attempt to answer.

An Entirely Different Discussion

A starting point is to distinguish fund-raising from stewardship. Fund-raising includes the ways we ask people for charitable support. These include pulpit announcements, letters, fliers, brochures, personal visits, pledge cards, weekly envelopes, and pledge statements. These are the "mechanics," essential to the conduct of the annual pledge drive, special appeals, and capital initiatives.

In contrast, stewardship involves the use of money in our lives overall: how much we believe God has blessed our lives, how much we earn, how much we save, what we buy with the money we have, and how we use all our resources to create a better world.

In some churches, stewardship is reflected in the practice of tithing. But that's not all. The remaining 90 percent of our income is to be used in ways that enable us to become the kind of people God wants us to become.

In traditional churches, unfortunately, the emphasis is often on fund-raising. Sharing in good measure as a hallmark of being a religious person appears less frequently. I believe focusing on the "how to" aspects of fund-raising are counterproductive, creating low-level and same-level giving among two-thirds or more of the members of many congregations.

Fund-raising appeals in church can also appear similar to appeals made by secular organizations. The ubiquitous campaigns of colleges and universities, hospitals, private schools, and other nonprofit organizations, however, are professional and sophisticated. They can make church appeals appear considerably less polished. For example, high-level donors to the symphony in a major city are entitled to dinner in an expensive restaurant with a favorite member of the orchestra. Other secular organizations also offer dazzling benefits or prizes. This is heady competition for the local parish.

A church's encouragement for parishioners to increase charitable giving can also be ineffective in comparison to the billions of dollars spent by the American advertising industry. As noted, the greatest obstacle to stewardship is the desire of people to live the good life. Robert Wuthnow summarizes this attitude with his observation that "respectability is the hallmark of the middle-class church, and the tokens of respectability include fine dress, attractive transportation, capacious homes, well-educated children, and successful careers."[1]

In some churches, Jesus' teachings about wealth are taken to heart, and parishioners are called to lead lives that go against the grain of the prevailing consumer culture. All too often, however, Wuthnow suggests that "churches say nothing at all about the material life, except to voice an occasional jab at the worship of mammon, adding hastily that there is nothing wrong with money as long as we do not love it too much."[2]

Creating an Effective Church

An essential element in making the annual pledge drive obsolete is church leaders having the courage to challenge congregants to examine the way they lead their lives. Robert Wuthnow also addresses this issue by noting, "The role of the church should be to challenge middle-class parishioners to lead unconventional lives of dedication, service, and sacrifice—to present an alternative view."[3]

He then adds forcefully, "If churches are to emerge from their present crisis, they must come to a clearer understanding of their role and ministry in relation to the middle class. Efforts to assist the downtrodden and the disadvantaged and to speak for greater justice on their behalf can succeed only if the middle class itself is challenged in ways that have seldom been seen in recent decades."[4]

The extent to which clergy and lay leaders are courageous in urging congregants to live a religious life will vary from congregation to congregation. How confident are congregational leaders in raising this issue to the church community? How receptive is the congregation likely to be? Would this kind of talk make parishioners angry? If so, should the topic be avoided altogether?

Equally important is the matter of how willing church leaders them-selves are to consider a greater commitment to the religious life and to the church. Are clergy and lay leaders willing to provide a "do what I do" example to others? If the leadership is unwilling to make a commitment to the challenges and occasional rigors of the religious life, it will be dif-ficult, if not impossible, to create this commitment throughout the con-gregation.

Churches have many options in helping parishioners lead lives of greater spirituality and commitment. Scripture is a traditional and pow-erful tool, and the Bible contains hundreds of references regarding the use and misuse of money. Many find great meaning in Scripture. Yet Peter Gomes, minister of Harvard's Memorial Church, has also noted, "Much of what the Bible has to say about wealth, riches, money, or earthly treasure is not what many Christians . . . want to hear."[5]

Beyond Scripture, churches have many other ways to engage contem-porary churchgoers in the discussion about money, some of which may be particularly appealing to younger generations. For example, the Voluntary Simplicity movement has become socially acceptable in recent years. The emphasis of this movement is a "more is less" approach to life, not only in regard to material possessions, but also how people allocate their daily hours to issues that hold the greatest meaning.

A study conducted by Juliet Schor of the Harvard Business School resulted in the finding that the average American today works *one full month* more per year than a generation ago.[6] Evening and weekend work is also more common. According to the respondents in Schor's study, 70 percent said they had little time or energy left over for other things [including church] when they came home from work. These are the peo-ple for whom the church can offer hope—people who are ground down by the daily routine and who see their lives slipping away day by day.

The voluntary simplicity movement is nontheological, but it can hold religious significance for people seeking a balance of solace and commit-ment in their lives. The voluntary simplicity movement is often associ-ated with the book *Your Money or Your Life* by Joe Dominguez and Vicky Robin.[7] Many mainline churches now offer programs on living a simple life based on these principles. The theological issue is not merely how we handle money, but rather the issue is the lives we lead.

Contemporary churchgoers might also emulate the Shakers of the nineteenth century who attempted to create heaven on earth based on stunning yet simple designs for furniture, buildings, clothing, and everyday items. Beyond basic needs, Shakers believed that most things on earth were superfluous.

The Willow Creek Community Church has developed a "Good $ense Ministry Kit" that addresses these very issues. The kit is described as a tool for helping the church "relieve the crushing stress and anxiety caused by consumer debt, restore marriages torn by conflict over money, and heal the wounded self-esteem and shattered confidence resulting from poor financial decisions. Most significantly, a Good $ense Ministry can be used by God to remove stumbling blocks to spiritual growth. . . . The result is a congregation whose finances—and lives—are characterized by grace, joy, and freedom."[8]

These various practices do not mean that religious people figuratively wear sackcloth and ashes to demonstrate their religious devotion. These movements are culturally and socially acceptable, even fashionable, and allow people to re-order their life priorities and the use of financial resources. These movements do not imply the social stigma of moving down a rung on the economic ladder. Rather, they lead to a better life, unencumbered by an ever-greater amount of consumer goods, and characterized by a focus on those things that carry the greatest meaning.

Many families, for example, have reconsidered gift giving at Christmas and other holidays. Instead of purchasing expensive gifts, some are making charitable donations in honor or memory of family members. This practice often includes the children of the family, who are taught the value and purpose of sharing life's bounty with others.

Regardless of theology or denomination, churches can create myriad opportunities for parishioners to examine the use of money in their lives, and to utilize their resources in ways that make the world a better place. These opportunities allow the church to discuss money without asking people for it, and are important aspects of the true meaning of stewardship.

Viewing stewardship in this manner is a "real life" ministry that addresses parishioners' day-to-day concerns. An important element of programs on simple living and effective money management is that they are "safe" for people to attend. These programs do not hint that people have mismanaged their money, nor is attendance a public admittance of that fact. These subjects are interesting in themselves and apply to people of all ages and economic circumstances.

A Higher Calling

Kortright Davis is an Episcopal priest and professor of theology at Howard University. In his book, *Serving with Power*, he addresses these life issues in a straightforward manner. He writes, "The presence of cultural comfort zones in our congregations may well be a serious indictment against what we claim to be all about. Does the church really take itself seriously? Does its membership live by the norms and values which it seeks to espouse for the common good?"[9]

Mainline faiths have been criticized for abandoning the concept of discipleship and substituting membership instead. Membership implies a type of belonging, but with no inherent responsibility to make a particular institution better or stronger. For example, people can become members of museums, various clubs, and a plethora of secular organizations. On becoming a member, little more is required.

Discipleship is an entirely different concept; it implies a commitment and ongoing involvement. I had the honor of hearing Kortright Davis preach, and in his sermon he proclaimed, "God does not set us free to leave us alone. The religious life is not casual and convenient."

What About All Those Poor People in the Church?

In my work with one mainline congregation, clergy and lay leaders frequently reminded me of the sizable number of poor people in the church. The week before I visited this congregation, the denomination's magazine printed a letter from a church member who claimed she was uncomfortable there, "because it is a rich people's church." As the saying goes, there is reality and there is the perception of reality.

I have been astonished to discover the perceptions that church leaders hold in regard to parishioners' income. In more than one instance, church leaders claimed that almost half of middle-class congregants earned less than $25,000 a year. Some of these leaders believed the church was being "heavy-handed" in asking so many poor people to give at all!

Clergy and lay leaders may believe there are indeed many poor people in church, and that a call to increased charitable giving is a lofty sentiment that does not reflect reality. The cost of living is ever higher. People work longer hours just to stay even. Those who have retired are living on fixed incomes. (Though a large group of seniors were not present in a church when I visited because they were on a European tour!) While some families may be getting ahead, others have lost purchasing power. People just don't have the money to give to the church, or anywhere else, for that matter.

This is a valid point for some families. I often ask clergy and lay leaders how many poor people are in the congregation. How many are unemployed? How many live without health insurance? How many cannot afford to take their children to the dentist? How many are eligible for public assistance, collect food stamps, or live in subsidized housing? These indicate poverty.

People who own homes, drive late model cars, buy their children TVs, stereos, and video game players, and travel are not poor. However, in the church's eyes, they are often viewed as unable to contribute proportionally.

Peter Gomes addresses the issue of charitable giving, whatever our circumstances. He writes, "Charity is enjoined upon each of us, not simply upon the rich, or upon those who can be said to be able to afford it."[10]

If your congregation has a sizable number of people who are living in or near poverty, then the stewardship question becomes, "What are the obligations of those who have more?" In some churches, parishioners are asked to fast for a certain number of meals each month and give the equivalent in cash to the church. This money goes into a discretionary fund that is available to those in the church who are struggling financially. Quite often, these discretionary funds contain large amounts of money. The members of the church believe it is their obligation to support one another in time of need.

In 1967, the Reverend Dr. Martin Luther King, Jr. wrote:

> A gulf has created conditions that permit necessities to be taken from the many to give luxuries to the few; and has encouraged small-hearted men to become cold and conscienceless so that, like Dives before Lazarus, they are unmoved by suffering, poverty-stricken humanity.[11]

In your church, do you believe that parishioner's attitudes toward money address the disparity that King describes so vividly? Are parishioners challenged about living the good life while others suffer? Are congregants encouraged to put more than a one-dollar bill in the collection plate? These issues lie at the heart of stewardship—not the maintenance of the institutional church.

This brings us back to the traditional stewardship approach that I believe falls short—asking parishioners to pay the church's bills. This approach literally puts blinders on parishioners in terms of what money is supposed to accomplish at church, how we use our resources to build lives of faith, and particularly how we assist others who are in greater need.

Middle-class citizens have been criticized for retreating into their careers and private lives, leaving the less fortunate to fend for themselves. Churches should challenge this attitude that may exist among large segments of middle-class parishioners. Is that not the role of the church in these times?

Mark Vincent, the publisher of the *Generous Giving Newsletter,* has identified this issue in a slightly different, but compelling way. He writes, "The threshold of what makes us uncomfortable lowers as assets increase."[12] As we gain in material things, are we less likely to engage aspects of life that are inconvenient or disorderly, and do we find ourselves avoiding our larger responsibilities? Does the church foster the notion of material comfort by allowing the good life to go unchallenged?

It is important to acknowledge that "high demand" churches encourage the tithe from people at all income levels. This is particularly true in inner-city and ethnic churches. Many of these churchgoers are certainly less affluent than their suburban counterparts. By asking them to give, churches respect congregants by honoring their capability. Churches should not act as the protectors of people's pocketbooks. People can decide how they wish to spend their own money, and a patronizing attitude from the church is not helpful.

I often meet people who tithe from across all income levels. I ask them what they gave up in order to give 10 percent of their income to the church. Most look at me quizzically, as though they don't understand the question. They don't believe they have denied themselves anything. Their attitude is just the opposite. They believe their lives have been immeasurably enriched. Having given up something is just not part of their consciousness.

During the past two years I worked with the stewardship committee of a church in planning how its efforts should go forward. This committee has six members. When I began meeting with this group, the custom was to take the first ten minutes to permit a committee member to describe how he or she came to tithe. It didn't dawn on me until the third month that they all tithed. These people have a different life imperative. They are eager to get together each month, and I look forward to being with them. Being in their presence has been an extraordinary gift to me. Among their ranks are a doctor, a lawyer, an investment advisor, a computer programmer, a retired teacher, and a freelance writer who made $25,000 last year. When I began working with this committee, I thought I would come in and "show them the way" that stewardship might play out in the congregation. Instead, they provided me a glimpse into a world that I had not seen so close up, a perspective for which I am deeply grateful.

Let us now summarize the ways in which mainline churches can make the annual pledge drive obsolete.

1. Raise the expectations of giving among the leadership of the church.

If the minister(s) and visible lay leaders are not generous in their own giving, it will be almost impossible to convince others to be generous. The standard for anyone wishing to assume a leadership role should be the tithe, a plan to tithe within a three-year period, or some level of proportional giving.

2. Increase the expectations of giving among newcomers.

Whatever the denomination, I believe potential new members should be informed that the expectation of giving is similar to leadership in the church, noted above. People are more open to suggestion when they join a church than at any other time. They are eager to become part of the congregation. They wish to be a meaningful part of a meaningful church. Their financial commitment will help ensure this.

Church leaders should communicate that this congregation takes the religious life seriously and wishes to create committed souls. Churches that are ambiguous about charitable giving or leave parishioners without guidance will create lukewarm members. Churches that perpetuate a "we don't talk about money" attitude will find that new members begin by giving little and are likely to establish a low-giving pattern for as long as they are in the church.

Don't worry about current members who joined the church when giving expectations were less. The goal is to increase the number of new congregants who are unafraid to tell others of the importance of their commitment to the church and to their spiritual lives. Bringing in new members at higher gift levels is the most effective way to change an existing culture of low-level and same-level giving.

3. Don't even think about conducting a congregational survey!

In my experience, congregational surveys "to find out what people think" are rarely worth the time and effort, and they can actually be quite harmful. A major shortcoming is that surveys are usually anonymous. It is difficult to determine whether respondents are active members or those who take little role in the church and are poorly informed about the issues. Thus, respondents' views are not equal, but they are often tallied and interpreted as being so. Also, even though surveys may contain a variety of issues on which to comment, they often end up being a referendum on the minister.

Contributing to the church in full measure is at the heart of a religious life and a community of faith. It is not a matter of "let's find out what people think." Leaders should lead. Clergy and lay leaders should acknowledge their leadership roles and declare that charitable giving is a core element in a life of faith. This message should be communicated to the congregation as an integral part of membership.

A congregational survey suggesting that parishioners increase their charitable giving will result in people saying that no one could possibly do this. What they are saying is that they, themselves, would not consider it, and they want to make that decision for everyone else, as well. These responses will weaken the resolve of the leadership, and the voices of the least generous will prevail.

Leadership in the Church

I would like to pause briefly to discuss the role of leadership in the congregation. George Barna's surveys indicate that only 5 percent of senior ministers say they have the gift of leadership. Most pastors believe they were neither called to nor divinely equipped for that post. Most ministers view themselves as teachers and put as little time into leadership activities as they feel they must in order to get by.[13]

A similar attitude exists among laypeople who hold leadership roles in church. Rarely do board members or trustees view themselves as leaders of the church. Rather, they view themselves as facilitators and mediators.

As an example, in a church newsletter, I read, "Your deacons and staff work hard. Please understand that the deacons receive many suggestions. For every person who wants announcements at the beginning of the service, another wants announcements at the middle or the end. For every person who wants to conclude worship within one hour, another hates to be rushed and doesn't want to exclude any of the important elements. We continually strive to compromise."

While this newsletter column addressed only Sunday worship, it demonstrates the role that church leaders often play—balancing the competing preferences, desires, whims, and demands that parishioners present. Clergy and lay leaders are sometimes hesitant to make even minor decisions, concerned that a segment of the congregation might be angered, that only a committee can make that decision, or that the minister has no authority in that area.

I've known ministers who would not make a decision that involved as little as $200. A subtle but very real aspect of congregational leadership is the desire to keep everyone happy—a fruitless and impossible task.

I also heard a board chair say, "We have over 40 committees in this church, and all seem to have equal value. About the best the board can do is tweak things that are already in place." Another board member from a different church said, "We are unsure of the loyalty of people to the congregation, and so we try not to offend anyone." One of her colleagues added, "How we do things around here is incrementalism personified. The pace is painstakingly slow."

This is not a book about church leadership per se, but effective leadership is a primary element in creating and maintaining vital congregations. All too often the prophetic voices are silenced by the established order—the routine of the church and its many requirements for approval.

I urge clergy, lay leaders, and people in the pews to define what effective leadership truly means in their own congregations. Now, let us return to the subject of stewardship and charitable giving.

4. Congregational leaders should be willing to take some heat for their stand.

Of course, not everyone in the congregation will heed the call to increased giving. Clergy and lay leaders are likely to hear a number of complaints. Do not let disgruntled members deter you from your resolve! My experience is that the most vocal complaints will come from those who *give* the least, not those who *have* the least. The whiners, complainers, naysayers, and freeloaders are not the ones who will lead the church to a promising future.

In contrast, those who already give the most will welcome the encouragement to increased generosity. These church pillars not only contribute the most, but they also ask the least in return. (This is why it is fine for the minister to know what people in the church contribute. Ministers usually do not give preferential treatment to higher-level donors because these people do not want preferential treatment.) High-level donors are often the most supportive of the minister, despite his or her flaws, and contribute in numerous ways beyond their monetary gifts. These are the generous and committed souls that churches can and should produce.

The religious life does not come easy, and it is not cheap. Churches that set the bar high in terms of membership and charitable giving will find that people strive to achieve the standard. They will be proud of themselves for doing so. Churches that set the bar too low exhibit disrespect for themselves and their parishioners.

It is important to recognize that low-income people require the opportunity to give. A minister in an affluent congregation once told me that at potluck meals, those who have the least invariably bring the most food. Giving is a matter of honor. Permit people of all income levels this dignity.

5. Recognize that changing attitudes toward giving is a long-haul proposition.

A major theme of this book is that attitudes toward money in the church may be the result of decades of history and tradition. Many congregations have a history of low-level and same-level giving, and this culture will not change overnight. Clergy and lay leaders should chart a steady course and expect that it will take two to three years for established parishioners to get over the initial shock of higher expectations. A period of grumbling about expectations will follow, and additional time will be required for the congregation to settle into a new order of things. Be patient, but persistent! Take delight in small gains, never lose your enthusiasm for God's work, pretend to be wearing a suit of armor when slights come your way, and hold steady to your course!

As noted, the core issue is not money. The essential issues are the lives we lead, the nature and character of the church, and what it means to be a faithful congregation. Clergy and lay leaders who engage people in a meaningful religious life will not worry about money. An added benefit is that churches that don't worry about money take more risks, and churches looking for new ways to serve are vastly more interesting to be a part of!

6. Know where you're starting from.

It is important for all congregants to see the pledge/gift figures. (This is not a list of gifts or pledges by name, even though some churches do provide this information.) Congregations need to establish baseline figures, which include:

—A list of every gift, from highest to lowest

—The number of pledging households

—The total amount pledged

—The median pledge

—The number of new members

—The number and amount of new gifts/pledges

—The number of nonpledging households (Many churches are likely to have 15 percent or more of active families that do not pledge or give, and these people must be included in the calculations to gain an accurate portrait of giving as a whole.)

These basic arithmetic calculations are an extremely important baseline in "keeping score" year by year. *Do not publish the average pledge!* This widely used figure diminishes parishioners who give the most, and elevates those who give the least. In fact, it rewards non-donor households the most. This is just the opposite of what we should be doing!

The median pledge (half above, half below) is a more accurate measure. In many congregations, the annual median pledge is between $250 and $500, or $5 to $10 per week, while the average pledge (thanks to high-level donors) might be $1,000. Thus, the average pledge is correct mathematically, but it conveys congregational giving inaccurately. The congregation should be provided an accurate accounting of its giving patterns on a regular basis.

A congregation's figures will reflect, "skewed giving." This means a small number of parishioners give a disproportionate share. As noted, 25 percent of congregants may give as much as 70 percent or more of the total amount raised. In attempting to increase giving, resist the temptation to suggest, "People who give less will just have to give more." This will not happen. The bottom two-thirds of donors may remain low-level givers for the remainder of their days in the congregation, and perhaps their days on earth. Their lack of giving may have little to do with how much money they have or don't have. No compelling mission statements, visions, rhetoric, or appeals from the church are likely to change their minds. The unfortunate fact is that many families, churchgoers or not, have no interest in charitable giving.

Keeping accurate figures is not a complicated task. Church database programs are readily available, and calculating standard percentages and statistics are standard features. Spreadsheet programs are also effective in tracking financial patterns. When a congregation sends me pledge figures in the mail in paper form, I use a calculator to do simple analyses. Determining this baseline data is basic arithmetic and easily obtained. Whenever possible, I prefer to review a ten year summary of giving figures.

7. Don't keep everyone in the dark.

In my experience with churches, the higher the level of secrecy around pledge figures, the lower the level of giving. In my view, the minister(s), board chair, and those involved in stewardship should have access to the giving records of parishioners. These key church leaders bear the responsibility not only of the church, but for the spiritual welfare of congregants, as well. Keeping secret records serves only one segment of the congregation—those who give the least. High levels of secrecy also do not permit the minister to express appreciation to those of modest means who support the church in ample measure. Thus, an opportunity for ministry is lost. What purpose is served by this practice?

8. Assess the attitudes of the congregation in terms of saving and spending.

Core elements of this book are our attitudes toward money at church and in our personal lives. This includes the endowment, which is addressed in chapter 10. The congregation needs to be involved in the discussion about how money flows in and out of the church, and the highest and best use of it. Are line items in the budget similar each year because the pledge drive is expected to raise the same amount each year? If so, how does the church ever begin a new ministry? Under what circumstances does the church save, and how much is necessary for that proverbial rainy day? Is there such a thing as saving too much money? What proportion of the church's resources is spent on the congregation, and what proportion goes to mission and outreach beyond the church's four walls?

Unfortunately, most churches bring up the subject of money only when they ask parishioners for it. The larger issues just noted are too infrequently discussed in the congregation as a whole.

9. Don't use the annual operating budget as the centerpiece of charitable giving.

At the risk of being repetitious, the expenses of running a church are not wellsprings of charitable giving. It doesn't matter what things cost, as long as expenditures are not excessive. Charitable giving is not an issue of how much money a church needs, but rather what we share to create and sustain lives of faith. I rarely review the budget in my own church, because I believe we should be raising and spending more! I give to my church because it does things that are important. I don't care how much the church pays for utilities, insurance, or other line items in the budget.

10. Cultivate attitudes of excellence and urgency.

In most areas of human endeavor, excellence is encouraged. We strive to do well in our work, careers, and other pursuits. We encourage our children to do well in school. We set high standards.

Excellence should be the standard in church, as well. Nothing is so disheartening as being trapped in irrelevant meetings, taking interminable periods of time to accomplish simple things, and having issues tabled for months on end. Many churches "wait for the right time" to do something, or believe they cannot act until all the money is in hand to initiate a particular project. This is a surefire formula for a church to lose its best and most talented people, who will seek more meaningful roles elsewhere.

11. Recognize that knowledge is power.

A significant reason churches struggle with financial issues is that clergy and lay leaders do not understand the nature and character of the organizations they serve. I find this a curious and distressing phenomenon.

In most aspects of our lives, if we are curious about a particular subject, we'll go to the library, search online, or call someone to see what we might find out. This seems a commonsense way of gaining knowledge, information, or insight concerning the subject at hand. The range of subjects people explore is limitless, of course, from everyday things like backyard birds and the stars at night, to faraway places, peoples, and cultures.

This natural expectation of learning is frequently absent at church. For example, when laypeople are elected or appointed to leadership roles in the church, some of which carry significant responsibility, they are provided little orientation or training. Lay leaders are usually unaware of books, journals, articles, or other literature that is readily available. To complicate the matter, I have found church leaders resistant to exploring the subject of church life and ways, even when they know these resources are readily available.

The result is that well-intentioned church leaders make decisions based on what they perceive to be common sense, instinct, or tried-and-true methods of the past. Or, they are comfortable making decisions only within a narrow range of issues. Along with the operating budget always being tight, this creates leaders who become caretakers rather than visionaries.

Lack of training and orientation for an important job in the secular world would never be tolerated. Lay leaders would rarely make decisions in their professional roles with so few resources or so little data. In fact, they would find these working conditions intolerable. Yet this is commonplace in church.

12. Pay the highest possible salaries to the minister(s) and church staff.

In my view, salary guidelines formulated by mainline denominations inadvertently limit clergy and staff compensation, making it difficult for religious professionals to negotiate equitable salaries. This subject is discussed at greater length in chapter 8. Excellence in leadership is not expensive, it is a bargain. Whenever possible, churches should exceed recommended salary guidelines for staff at all levels.

Beyond salary, one or more congregational leaders will need to become knowledgeable about benefit packages, health insurance, pension programs, and continuing education for staff. While many denominations oversee pension and insurance programs, the rules and regulations are ever changing.

13. Seek committed leaders who believe their role is not to please everyone.

Today, many "church shoppers" and churchgoers alike are viewed (and criticized) as coming to church with a consumer attitude of "what's in it for me?" Churches that are on a plateau or in decline are eager to engage newcomers, and they often display an attitude of how they can meet the needs of all. The orientation is one of what the church offers, as in, "We hope you like the minister, the sermons, the choir, the church's programs, the refreshments at coffee hour, and life here at the church."

George Barna's surveys indicate that nonchurched people "expect a church to conform to the will, needs or interests of the individual person. Nonchurched people would define a healthy, compelling church as one that does whatever is necessary to satisfy the tangible needs of the person. . . . Few nonchurched adults think of the church as the pivotal player in this drama with the attender following a prescribed role for a predetermined purpose."[14] In my experience, people who are members often view the church similarly.

Strong and healthy congregations are clear in who they are and what they do. They are also clear in what they do not do. They do not attempt to appeal to everyone. All are welcome, but becoming a member carries a commitment that is clearly stated. In some churches, people are not allowed to become members until they have spent sufficient time in the church and understand the expectations of membership fully, including the commitment of time and charitable giving.

Many strong churches also focus on how members serve together as a congregation—not on how the church as an institution serves its members. Clergy and lay leaders in these congregations believe that on the sailing vessel that is the church, everyone takes an oar and rows. There are not separate compartments for sailors rowing down in the hold, while passengers sit at leisure on the upper decks—especially passengers who got on board without buying a ticket!

14. Provide opportunities to discuss charitable giving on a regular basis.

Money is an issue that parishioners deal with every day of their lives. We may have more money at one time, less at another. People's fortunes rise and fall. I believe churches should provide ongoing forums, speakers, classes, and seminars that draw people together and assist them in using the resources at their command to create meaningful lives. This is a far cry from the church asking for money. Engaging people in how their resources can be used to create a better world means the church acts as a true partner in traveling with parishioners on their religious journeys.

An excellent example of this approach comes from the Antioch Churches and Ministries, which provide individuals and families with "financial services in the following areas: accounting, budgets, taxes, mutual funds, financial planning, mortgages, trusts, pensions, IRAs, CDs, and insurance."[15] This church believes that money is an intensely spiritual issue, and that how people manage their material resources should be a public reflection of their faith.

I believe parishioners require assistance and support if they desire to make significant changes in their attitudes toward money, because it is easier to make significant life decisions in a group than alone. For example, dieting is easier if others are also doing it, as is physical exercise. Alas, our human nature allows us to delay things that are inherently good for us. A dose of spiritual (and financial) discipline would be a good thing for many souls.

15. Help parishioners find meaning in philanthropy.

Anyone at any income level can become a philanthropist. One of the brightest stars in the world of charitable giving was not wealthy at all. Oseola McCarty took in washing and ironing all her life. When she was eighty-five years old, she gave $150,000 to the University of Southern Mississippi for a minority scholarship fund. The photo of Oseola McCarty shown most frequently is one in which she holds a Bible in her hands. She was a church-going woman her entire life.

We are aided in our spiritual lives and made whole by what we give. When we do not share in proportion, some part of our hearts and souls begins to shrivel or become withered. This is incompatible with the religious life.

16. Ask: Who is served by all this?

The theologian Thandeka often asks this question of religious communities. Who is served by your church? The answer to this simple yet powerful question speaks volumes about whether the congregation is called to do God's work, or if it serves only its own members. People may need the comfort and respite of church as a sanctuary from distress—some frequently, others less so. But this cannot be a church's main focus. Churches are called to serve. Traditional churches often wish to transform social structures into becoming more justice oriented. Many newly formed churches focus their efforts on saving one person, one heart, and one soul at a time. Whom does your church serve that is truly in need? And whom does your church serve that already enjoys life's bounty?

Being a generous person or family is one of life's great privileges. Clergy, lay leaders, and people in the pews should all foster this notion. Those who are drawn to such a church will find themselves entering into and engaged by a culture of welcoming and sharing. What a wonderful church that is.

CHAPTER FIVE

Who Controls the Money?

If you don't like the way I'm handling the church's money, maybe you'd like to do it yourself.

A church treasurer in response to a parishioner's question

I recently received a phone call from a board member of a mainline church. She said that during the previous meeting, the board had considered two financial decisions. The first involved selling a gift of stock and depositing the proceeds in the bank. The second was to withdraw money from a separate account to fund a request from the Missions Committee. After some debate, the board concluded that it could deposit proceeds from the sale of stock, but did not have the authority to withdraw cash.

This, of course, raised an obvious question. If the governing body did not have the authority to withdraw money from the church's bank account, who did? The answer to this question provides a revealing glimpse into congregational life. Who makes financial decisions in your church?

In mainline congregations, individual parishioners may hold the position of treasurer, financial secretary, or investment advisor for years, perhaps decades, on end. These influential members can exert a powerful influence over the financial affairs of a church. Even questionable decisions made by these often (but not always) well-intentioned volunteers may go unchallenged because most parishioners do not want a confrontation.

In traditional churches, committees are also likely to make financial decisions. These include the finance committee, budget committee, investment committee, the governing board, and variations thereof. Church leaders may wish to assess whether Lyle Schaller's belief is correct that "the most gifted and the most deeply committed volunteers are 'creamed off' to serve on the governing board or to staff the finance committee or trustees. This reinforces the impression that governance, money, and real estate are the top priorities in congregational life."[1]

A Different View

Newly founded churches often do not use a committee structure. A major difference is that the founding minister sets the vision and direction of the congregation as a whole. He (more often than she) holds considerably more authority in determining the work of the church than in mainline faiths that use a model of congregational polity.

The organizational structure of newly formed churches may consist of teams with broad mandates, rather than standing committees. This helps avoid the "join the church and be put on a committee" approach that is prevalent in mainline congregations. Teams are sometimes referred to as "a church within a church," and each team works toward the mission and vision of the congregation.

These teams are not the fiefdoms sometimes found in mainline churches, committees whose membership goes relatively unchanged for long periods of time, and which can become closed cliques. Rather, teams are given broad responsibilities, are expected to involve new members as active partners, and have changing leadership. Their main purpose is to be continually vigilant in adjusting the life of the church to changing times.

Teams might be structured along the lines of the "Stability Triangle" proposed by author and church consultant Thomas Bandy. These include the Staff Team, the Human Resources Team, and the Administration Team.[2] My own view is that two teams might suffice: Administration and Finance, which oversees personnel and building issues; and Worship, Mission, Outreach, and Education. Each team would be given a portion of the budget to spend as they see fit. This would help phase out the line item budget, a giant step ahead for church boards that find themselves mired in debating $50 or $100 items. These teams would be granted considerable authority and permission to pursue the mission-driven goals of the congregation.

The team approach does not call for "offices" that carry specific job descriptions. Rather, roles that people assume are more fluid and are expected to evolve as the congregation continually adjusts to a changing world. This structure allows more flexibility, permits congregants (especially newcomers) a wider range of options for service, welcomes and values the ideas of newcomers, does away with the prevailing committee structure, and works as a powerful tool in developing leadership skills among the laity.

The new church model also relegates the board to a different role, far from the traditional governance model. Bandy describes this as the board "[looking] up from the ledger and the committee reports to see if the world is really changing because of the presence of their church."[3] In this model, the board is assigned the role of continually reassessing outreach opportunities, targeting missions, and ensuring high-quality initiatives. The board encourages unrestricted giving, as is the case in many congregations, but lets each team decide how best to use its own resources.

Lyle Schaller recommends: "A different model for staffing begins with a different perspective. Instead of focusing on what a staff person will do, this approach begins by asking what should happen. The focus is on outcomes, not inputs."[4] This staffing configuration is covered in greater detail in chapter 8, "The Cost vs. the Value of Religious Leadership."

I encourage mainline churches to consider the team approach. However, it would be a huge leap for many congregations. As suggested, church leaders all too often assume the role of caretakers, either by design or default, and they find themselves preserving an established church. Newcomers are expected to discover the church on their own rather than from evangelism on the part of members, and they are viewed more or less as replacements for those who have left. Church life continues as usual.

In contrast, a bedrock strategy of newly formed churches is identifying those who will be the new members of the future, devising strategies to reach them, and expecting newcomers to have transforming ideas for ministry once they arrive. New churches often use a broad type of program budgeting, allocating large portions of the budget to mission, evangelism, and ministry. This is an empowering, permission-granting model.

Existing Structures

If standing committees make financial decisions in your church, the governing body should analyze the makeup of these committees on an ongoing basis. Standing committees have a tendency to institutionalize habits that may or may not foster the well-being of the congregation as a whole. These habits can, for better or worse, carry forward for long periods of time. They become a familiar part of the prevailing culture, or "how we do things around here."

All too often, poor habits regarding the use of money are passed down from one generation to the next. It is entirely possible for a small number of church leaders to maintain financial policies almost indefinitely, even if these policies became ineffective long ago. The status quo in many churches has enormous staying power.

In his book *The Middle-Sized Church*, Lyle Schaller examines length of membership to devise an interesting "Four congregations in one" model in the traditional church.[5] Let's take a look at who these four groups are, then determine who controls the purse strings.

The Old Old-Timers These parishioners have been in the church for thirty years or more, and are usually the most elderly. Some remember the era in which women wore hats and gloves to church on Sunday morning. The distinguishing feature of this group is the memory of a previous pastor, usually one who was beloved. Some may believe the church's "Golden Age" was in the past.

The New Old-Timers This group has been involved in the church for fifteen to thirty years and often constitutes the leadership. Clergy often appreciate the dedication of this segment of the church population. However, Schaller suggests that opposition to new programs might also come from this group. Their attitude may be, "The church was good enough for us and our children, so why do we have to do all these new things (spend money) to please recent arrivals?"

The Old Newcomers These people have been around for five to fifteen years and may well be the impetus for change. They do not like run-down bathrooms and kitchens, musty basements where Sunday school classes are held, or other shortcomings that older members have gotten used to and find acceptable.

The New Newcomers These parishioners have known the church no other way than it currently is. Often the youngest, though not always, they have grown up in a world that offers high quality choices. They may join the Old Newcomers in not settling for less and in advocating for improvements in the church.

Two important questions arise from this model. The first is, "What percentage of the congregation falls into each category, and why?" The answer to this question will help reveal why churches may or may not attract newcomers, what the church has to offer each of these four segments of the population, and why churches may or may not retain members once they have joined. It is not a "given" that members will start out as New Newcomers and stay long enough to become Old Old-Timers. It is also an interesting exercise for church leaders to determine what brings each of these groups to church and what they find of value. Not everyone comes to church for the same reason.

A second question in regard to the length of time people have been members of a church, and more related to the subject of this book is, "Which group(s) controls the money?" When I asked this question recently, a gentleman replied, "You've overlooked one important group. At my historic church, there is a burying ground out back, and people who were buried there two hundred years ago still influence how money is saved and spent!" He also mentioned that two oil portraits of the stern-looking founders were on prominent display in the room where church business was conducted. "No matter where you are in that room," he added, "their eyes watch you, implying that not one dime should be spent unless absolutely necessary. In my church, the eighteenth and nineteenth centuries still loom large in the affairs of the congregation."

It is not a difficult task for clergy and lay leaders to analyze who controls money in a given congregation. In some instances, it may be key volunteers who hold influential views. In the case of the church board that didn't believe it could authorize a bank withdrawal, the answer may be less certain. No set formula exists to determine who controls the money, but a starting place includes age and term of office.

Generational Differences

As a general rule, older members of a congregation are likely to favor thrift and saving because they remember hard times and believe that saving money will help prevent these times from returning again. They believe in the institution of the church and are dedicated to its preservation, but they may be cautious regarding financial expenditures.

Younger parishioners are likely to be considerably more casual about spending interest income and even unrestricted principal because they grew up in more prosperous times. They believe that money spent can always be replaced, because this has been their life experience. Of course, many variations lie in between. An important element in a church reaching common understanding about money is determining the range of financial views among church leaders, and the extent to which each might prevail.

Let's return once again to Lyle Schaller, who adds another dimension to the issue of control in congregational life. This is whether a church looks to the future or to the past. He writes, "Orientation [to the past] is often reinforced when many of the current leaders have been in office for at least a decade, and some have been leaders for more than twenty years. While there are many exceptions to this generalization, the pattern of normal and predictable human behavior is that the older the person, and/or the longer that individual has been in the same office or position of leadership, the stronger the past orientation."[6]

If Schaller's view reflects the situation in your church, that is, if church leaders have held office for many years and are oriented toward the past, great diplomacy may be required in creating a new order. Longtime volunteers, regardless of age, might believe they have served the church faithfully, and feel they are being pushed aside.

An elderly woman once introduced herself as a new newcomer, and I certainly don't believe age is the true measure of a leader's effectiveness. I have had the honor of working with church pillars in their sixties, seventies, and in one instance a gentleman of eighty-two who wished to create a church of the future for their children and grandchildren. These living saints have the church's best interests at heart.

I have also worked with volunteers, both young and old, who have threatened to leave the church in protest, "and take all my friends with me," when changes in the established order were suggested. Unfortunately, some parishioners set their own interests above the church and can hold a congregation hostage. A prime example is a treasurer who will not divulge the giving records of the congregation. Removing such a person from office can be a very painful, though necessary, decision.

A Few Alternatives

Mainline congregations facing the issue of entrenched leadership have a number of options available to them. For example, a church in the Midwest requires one new member (of less than two years standing) on each committee of three persons or more. This policy is written into the church's bylaws and promotes continually renewed leadership. This prevents one group of parishioners from gaining inordinate control over the congregation's affairs, financial or otherwise.

Term limits are also a good policy, in which church officers serve for a certain period of time. A standard length of service is a three-year term, renewable one time for a total of six years. This is an effective policy only when church officers or committee chairs rotate off their respective groups when their terms are complete. Having a former chairperson retain a seat at the table is not a good idea. This rotating-off policy permits incoming leadership to chart new directions—something that would be difficult to do if former board chairs who initiated current practices remain part of the discussion.

Churches can also institute a policy of revolving leadership by appointing vice-chairs to key committees. These "leaders in training" assume the position of committee chair after a certain period of time. However, the governing body must be diligent in ensuring that emerging leaders who "learn the ropes" in this fashion do not perpetuate ineffective habits and traditions.

One final recommendation regarding leadership is a policy that does not permit individual parishioners to hold leadership positions on multiple committees. In most churches, a cadre of people constitutes the "pillars" and stalwarts. These dedicated congregants rise to the occasion whenever the church requires assistance. Ministers are eternally grateful for these people who care so deeply about the church. However, if the same people hold leadership roles in too many aspects of congregational life, the garnering of power is a likely result. All too often, this includes holding on to established traditions and an unwillingness to entertain new ideas, especially from younger members, newcomers, and those who "haven't paid their dues" by being around the church long enough.

For mainline churches in which a large number of long term leaders are unwilling to budge, assistance may be required from the judicatory, the denomination, or a church consultant.

Policies toward the use of money in church should be reviewed and updated as the life of the congregation progresses. Churches are not petrified forests, forever set in time. They are living entities. Times change, people come and go, and new opportunities for ministry continually present themselves. Or, a church might find its very existence threatened. The finances of a church require watchful eyes and skilled hands, a willingness to take some risks, and a diligence to ensure that ineffective policies are not carried forward.

If any one segment of the congregation retains control over the financial affairs of the church for lengthy periods of time, or if ambivalence reigns because no stated policies exist, money is likely to be hoarded rather than used for effective ministry. I do not believe a miserly attitude toward money, either in the church or in our personal lives, is how we define ourselves as people of faith.

Limiting Ministry Through Fiscal Responsibility

Healthy congregations . . . respond readily and often eagerly to new challenges in ministry, even when the money does not appear to be readily available to finance those new ventures.

Lyle Schaller[1]

The quotation above is one of my favorites from Schaller, and after using it during a seminar, I received a letter from a church treasurer. He wrote, "Any organization should know what to expect in receipts, so it does not overspend. Fiscal conservatism is conserving resources, avoiding risk, planning for the worst case, and thinking carefully about expenditures. Fiscal responsibility is crucial to the success of any organization, including the church."

I shared this observation with my colleague, the Reverend James McPhee, a denominational staff member with the United Methodist Church. His reply:

This is the issue I have been arguing throughout my pastoral career. Those who desire fiscal responsibility at all times are too risk-averse. They do not see the urgency of new mission and ministry. Their own experience may be of conserving financial resources instead of using money in active and constructive ways. I have experienced congregations (usually among the less affluent) in which the mission drives the giving. As we respond more fully to needs in our community, as we respond to God's call, the funds will follow these expressions. I testify that I have seen this happen time and time again.

The two views just presented about the use of money at church might fall into the categories of "liberal" and "conservative," but I'm not going to suggest that one is preferable to the other. Nor am I going to recommend that saving is better than spending, or that one view is right and the other is wrong. Churches are complex organizations, and simplistic definitions do not address myriad financial issues that arise. At times, churches should save, and at other times, they should spend.

A Brief Case Study

Let's take an example. I am familiar with a mainline church that was conducting a capital campaign for a building addition. The goal was $1.5 million. While the campaign was underway, a parishioner died and left the church a bequest of $250,000. This bequest was unrestricted, which meant the money could be designated for any purpose. The church board made the decision to allocate the money for the building addition.

This decision infuriated a group of congregants who believed the money should have been put into the endowment. This group left the church in anger over the board's decision. In considering the judgment of the church board, was applying $250,000 toward the building a "liberal" or "conservative" decision? Was it right or wrong? Was the decision a matter of spending or saving? Some argued that the money was spent, since it was paid to contractors. Others argued that the gift was an investment in the health and vitality of the church, and remained an asset.

What might your congregation do with a sizable amount of money that arrived in the form of an unexpected bequest? Some churches have existing policies in regard to bequests, but many do not. Should the governing board decide on a case-to-case basis? Should there be a congregational vote? If so, what if a congregation votes 55 to 45 percent, one way or the other, thus leaving almost half of parishioners on the "losing" side?

Three additional issues arose with the receipt of this gift. The first is a response that is out of proportion to the scale of the decision—people leaving the church. With a goal of $1.5 million, this church had a sizable budget and pledge drive. While $250,000 is a significant sum, should it be large enough to drive people from the church? If the decision had been to put this bequest into the endowment, would it really have made that much difference over the long haul?

Also overlooked in this squabble was the church having received the gift in the first place. Instead of a blessing, this generous gift became a source of conflict. Is this the way people of faith respond? This kind of pettiness shows up in the local grapevine (or newspaper headline), makes churches look foolish, warns potential newcomers to be wary, and discourages current parishioners from leaving their own wealth to the church.

Third, the church kept all the money for itself. Later in this chapter, an alternative is presented.

It bears repeating that clergy and lay leaders often project personal views about money onto the life of the church. In our personal lives, we anticipate a certain amount of income in a given period of time, and we attempt to spend accordingly. For most people, concern for the future is a significant issue. We hope to lead a comfortable life, put our children through college, and have sufficient funds on which to retire. We wish to invest our resources wisely. To spend money from accumulated assets or capital is considered imprudent. We would spend this money only in an emergency.

Congregational leaders often bring this view to church. However, churches operate with very different economic imperatives. In particular, they are not necessarily limited to a finite or predictable amount of money coming in. Churches often receive bequests, special gifts, and what is called "over the transom" money that unexpectedly appears from one source or another.

When unanticipated money comes in, clergy and lay leaders might view that extra sum in the same way they view their personal finances. They want to save it for the future, just in case. Thus, churches can save more than they need. A core issue, however, supersedes what is saved or spent. That issue is whether a spendthrift attitude becomes intractable in the life of the congregation.

My own bias is that many churches should spend more. Saving too much money creates congregations that are tentative and cautious, avoiding even small risks because preserving capital becomes the central focus. Congregational leaders should also be cognizant that sizable bank accounts all too often create a congregation of low-level donors. Parishioners may believe the church doesn't need their charitable support. Why should people give to the church when it already has plenty of money; or even worse, too much money?

Churches are not banks. Churches are communities of faith that are called to serve. Besides, I believe that money invested in vital ministries comes back in one form or another, often in greater measure. Money is much like love. The more we give, the more we receive in return. The Reverend Dale Galloway, a pastor and author of more than a dozen books, summarizes this in just five words: "Only what we share multiplies."[2]

In *The Church Growth Handbook*, author William Easum also addresses this issue by suggesting a "Law of Congregational Life." He states, "Churches, like people, are healthiest when they reach out to others rather than worry about themselves. Churches grow because they intentionally reach out; churches die because they dwell on their own internal problems."[3]

The Line Between Financial Responsibility and Financial Risk

Two important issues come into play regarding the effective use of money at church. The first is the spirit of God, what author Karen Fields describes as religion "full to overflowing with spectacular improbabilities."[4] Many clergy and lay leaders believe that when the Holy Spirit is present, all things are possible. Religious literature abounds with stories of churches taking on seemingly impossible tasks and succeeding in the face of overwhelming odds.

The practical souls at church, those charged with managing the budget and providing oversight of the church's financial affairs, might cast a more watchful eye on fiscal reality. To spend money too freely could jeopardize the financial health of the church. For every church that embarked on a risky venture and succeeded, another may have taken a similar risk and failed.

How are clergy and lay leaders to decide what a reasonable risk looks like? When does a reasonable risk become foolhardy? How does a congregation know when a ministry or outreach effort has made a difference? Let's take a look at a number of options that churches have available to them.

Reasonable Risks

The recommendations that follow are within reach of most congregations, though they may not realize it, and are based on money that has been raised and is available to spend. Some readers may feel that churches undertaking the variety of appeals that follow will be accused of "talking about money all the time." I believe a combination of these appeals is appropriate and justified, as religious communities are continually called to serve.

We might recall once again that economists, financial advisors, and observers of the spending habits of American citizens believe that most people could double their charitable giving and hardly notice the difference in their checkbooks. For example, if a middle-class family writes a check to the church each month for $50, would they really notice the difference if that check was for an additional $50? The deep well of charitable giving has barely been tapped.

Before summarizing a variety of reasonable risks, it is important to note that some ministries may have recognizable outcomes, and some may not. For example, I am familiar with an urban church that started an after-school program for children from a nearby low-income neighborhood. This program serves 30 children each weekday, from 2:30 to 5:00 P.M. It is run like a small nonprofit organization within the church (an example of the need for specialized staff) and reports to an advisory body. This church program has highly visible results.

In contrast, what is the value of a youth trip to a Habitat for Humanity site? My teenage son came back from a youth venture to a Habitat site, and his worldview had changed considerably. My wife and I, along with the parents of other teens, were enormously grateful to the church for providing this experience. Few other congregants, however, were aware of this, and might not perceive its value the way we did.

At times, congregations need to take a leap of faith in determining the benefits of outreach and mission efforts. Churches usually spend money prudently, and rarely invest in foolish ventures. It is not always possible to know the full extent or influence of a particular program or ministry. The important issue is the church being in a position to take advantage of opportunities that arise by utilizing the skill, talent, and courage of church leaders, and by having available financial resources.

I have seen congregations stalled in their tracks, unable to initiate even the smallest ministries because of a pervasive attitude of "we don't have the money." Let us see how we can prevent this from happening by summarizing some ventures that are within the reach of most communities of faith.

1. Mission and outreach in the budget

For many congregations, giving away 10 percent of the church's budget to mission is a bedrock principle. The church as an institution tithes. In the case of the church that received a $250,000 bequest during a building campaign, a better use of that money would have been a tithe from the capital campaign itself, giving away 10 percent of all money raised for new construction. This practice enables a congregation to gather and worship in good conscience in the building itself, because they have not spent only on themselves.

Many churches try to increase mission giving each year. For example, a federated Methodist/United Church of Christ congregation in Newton, Massachusetts, now has 29 percent of its budget going toward mission. The Memorial Drive Presbyterian Church in Houston gives away one dollar for the needs of the world for every dollar the church spends on itself. That policy is written into the church's bylaws. Would that all churches strive for this ideal!

Silvio Nardoni, a minister and attorney, articulated this view by noting, "Churches should have clear windows through which parishioners look out and engage the world, not mirrors which reflect only the needs of parishioners in the pews."

Greg Ligon is a Methodist minister and director of the Leadership Training Network, an organization that helps clergy and laypeople become effective church leaders. In a recent article, he articulates this point clearly. "The point of church growth is not to collect new people and cage them with church programs," he writes, "the Church exists to equip people in order to release them back into the world, grounded in truth and community, dangerous for the gospel."[5]

Later in the same article, Ligon adds, "Churches [like this] not only talk about but demonstrate a track record of discipleship on the streets. They don't measure success in the number of attendees in various church programs. Instead, they measure their effectiveness in reducing the crime rate of their community, bridging the economic divide of their city, and communicating to the world the reality of Christ's compassion in meeting immediate and eternal needs." Ligon is describing a concept called the "Equipping Church."

Reaching out to serve brings us back to the element of risk, and initiating new ministries even when the source of funds may not be readily available. I once heard Herb Miller, founder of Net Results (a church consulting firm and publisher), say, "Churches seldom die of taking risks. They often die of security—not instantly, but eventually."

Clergy, lay leaders, and people in the pews will exhibit different levels of risk tolerance toward financial matters. Whose views will hold sway? How do congregational leaders decide whether to make "conservative" or "liberal" financial decisions? To what extent do financial decisions have to be acceptable to a majority of the members of the congregation? Attitudes about financial issues vary from church to church. How will you assess the situation in your church?

Let us now return to other reasonable risks that churches can take to enhance their health and vitality.

2. Off-season giving

Many churches conduct a scaled-down version of the annual pledge drive in the season opposite the main appeal. For example, if the annual pledge drive is held in the fall, the mini-appeal is held in the spring. Many variations are possible. The most frequent is a goal of approximately 10 to 15 percent of the annual budget, equally divided for mission, care of the property, and enhancement of ministry in the church.

This is a particularly effective method of encouraging generosity. The special appeal is also a means of getting away from the long-held tradition of seeking "large dollar" financial support only one time each year during the annual pledge drive. The goal can be announced from the pulpit and in the church newsletter some weeks in advance, with a special collection scheduled on a particular Sunday. These appeals should have a specific dollar goal.

It is essential that a dollar goal be specified, rather than a message of, "Anything you can give will be appreciated." The notion of "anything is appreciated" gives permission for people to put a one-dollar bill (or spare change) in the collection plate and feel they have responded adequately.

3. Special appeals

Smaller appeals can be sprinkled throughout the year as the need arises, and are usually for lesser dollar goals. Appeals of this nature are most effective for mission, or when the money is not used for the operation of the church. Appeals can certainly be spontaneous. For example, a special appeal might support someone from the congregation who is serving in a mission somewhere in the world, who happens to be home for a visit. A minister or worship leader might announce, for example, that the church would like to raise an extra $1,000 to $2,000 this morning for this special mission. In larger churches, the amount may be much greater.

I recall attending services at an Episcopal church with about 150 people present, and the minister said he had been moved by the plight of survivors of a hurricane in Central America. He was going to send a check for $1,000 for relief efforts, and he invited parishioners to join him. This was a spontaneous request. Two weeks later, I read in the church newsletter that $16,000 had been given that Sunday morning. This amount was matched by an anonymous donor, for a total of $32,000.

Special appeals can also be held for local families in need, for specifically designated organizations that serve the less fortunate, for community or civic projects, or for a wide array of other local or regional needs. It is perfectly acceptable for these appeals to have a "build up" time by being announced in the newsletter or from the pulpit some weeks in advance.

Special appeals are particularly effective at the holidays of Christmas, Thanksgiving, and Easter, when people are mindful of their own blessings. All special appeals should have a specific dollar goal. I recommend that special appeals encourage people to write checks of between $50 and $1,000 on the spot. Clergy and lay leaders may be surprised at what people will give when asked.

Not everyone will respond to every appeal, of course, but many will. I believe congregations take great pride in what they accomplish collectively, and smaller appeals that are successful in reaching dollar goals will instill a sense of confidence that people can do great things in God's name.

4. Church programs

A church's ongoing programs may include outreach efforts like building houses for Habitat for Humanity, prison ministries, food drives, or other initiatives that involve both financial support and volunteer time. Some churches include the costs of these outreach efforts in their operating budgets, while others conduct separate appeals for financial support throughout the church year.

These programs tend to attract dedicated followers who give generously to support the church as a whole, and to the project in which they are involved. These parishioners are an inspiration. They exist in all congregations, come in all ages, and represent a wide spectrum of economic backgrounds.

Sometimes these programs are "big ticket" items and involve parishioners traveling to missions in foreign countries. Many congregations sponsor foreign missions and raise large sums outside the operating budget for their ongoing support. In my experience, raising money for mission is not a zero sum game in relation to the annual pledge drive. In fact, the opposite is the case. When missions are successful, annual giving often increases.

A large-scale appeal for mission, however, may be more effective if it does not compete with the annual pledge drive, and is held in the opposite season. Some churches do conduct concurrent appeals, with parishioners being asked to make one gift to the church and another to mission. In such cases, clergy and lay leaders should monitor giving figures carefully to determine if concurrent appeals compete with one another. If so, rescheduling one appeal to a different season is a possible solution.

I believe successful, ongoing outreach and mission projects are excellent antidotes to the commonly held attitudes of "people are already giving as much as they possibly can," and "no one around here has any money to give." There is nothing like success to dispel this notion!

5. Emergency appeals

Many churches respond to appeals when disaster strikes. Examples include natural disasters in this country or in faraway places. The terrorist attacks on the World Trade Center and the Pentagon brought destruction and loss of life closer to home than ever before, and over $1.5 billion in charitable gifts flowed in during just a few months time. Quite often, church members who are physicians or health care professionals organize trips to disaster sites, taking volunteers, medical supplies, and financial contributions with them. Other disasters occur in the local community when a family has experienced a serious illness or a tragedy of one kind or another.

I believe churches rise to the occasion and their lights shine most brightly at these times. Time and again, I have observed clergy, lay leaders, and people of many faiths engage in acts of extraordinary compassion that indicate the presence of a living God. In these instances, money is rarely an issue.

Many churches have utilized the five charitable giving options listed above. This demonstrates a critically important concept: the availability of money and the capacity of people to give are not the issues. The money is out there. The money has always been out there, even in the most difficult times. The key issue is the amount that we as religious people keep for ourselves, and the measure we share with those who have not experienced God's bounty. This is a bedrock principal of stewardship.

Stewardship is not asking people for money, though this is the common perception. Rather, the task for clergy and lay leaders is twofold: to create a climate in which parishioners will speak with others about the role that charitable giving plays in their lives; and to encourage parishioners to engage in behaviors that cultivate generosity and sharing as the means to a fulfilling religious life. Stewardship is not a matter of asking for money in more clever ways. As my colleague Michael Reeves noted, "Stewardship is not an event, but a process."

Now that we've covered the less-risky approaches, let's turn our attention to more adventuresome initiatives.

CHAPTER SEVEN

High-risk Ventures

Money? No problem!

Chapter title in the book, Churchquake! by Peter Wagner

L et's look at two examples of churches that took high risks, and the results that ensued.

I Might Not Get Paid?

The Reverend Robert Hoffman began his ministry at the First Lutheran Church in Turnersville, New Jersey, in 1977. When he arrived, he found a leaky roof, an organ in disrepair, a dirt parking lot that became a sea of mud when it rained, a $26,000 loan payment that was due, and the church's membership in decline. Hoffman also noted that the church had given nothing in "benevolences," or mission, for a number of years. The congregation's leaders were gravely concerned about the future of the church.

When board members asked Hoffman what the church should do, he replied, "We begin by giving away 10 percent of the operating budget to benevolences. If we cannot live faithfully, I cannot be your pastor." Board members were taken aback. Their immediate reaction was that the church could not possibly do this. Hoffman asked church leaders to take a few weeks to think and pray about this important decision before they met again.

At the board meeting the following month, the chairman said reluctantly, "Well, Pastor, I guess we can give it a try. But if we do, we may not have enough money to pay you." Hoffman was not unprepared for this response. He replied, "Okay. We'll do benevolences first, but I want to be paid second, before any of the church's expenses." The board agreed.

The church gave away 10 percent of the operating budget that year. Church leaders also put a fresh coat of paint on a little-used parsonage, and sold it to pay off the $26,000 loan on schedule.

"At first, parishioners thought I was nuts," Hoffman said. "They didn't quite know what was happening. As the weeks and months went by, word got out about what we had done, and we began to attract visitors. The church began to grow."

"We also decided to increase our benevolences by 1 percent each year," Hoffman added. "At the five-year mark we initiated two Sunday services because the sanctuary was full to overflowing, and at eight years we had to enlarge the building. We became a church that didn't focus on institutional maintenance, but gave beyond itself. Today, twenty-five years later, that church remains one of the strongest parishes in the synod. It has continued to grow over the years. After I finished my term as senior minister, church leaders continued the traditions we began. They hired subsequent pastors who were in tune with that model of ministry."

"I would never have put my salary at risk," Hoffman added, "if I hadn't been a student minister at St. Paul's Lutheran Church in Holly, New Jersey, where I worked with a group of truly extraordinary people. When I was there in the early 1970s, the church received a $10,000 bequest. Instead of keeping the money, the congregation decided to give the money to other churches to help support student ministers."

"A few years later," Hoffman continued, "the church received a bequest of $1.3 million. They put $400,000 into a building project, and gave away the remaining $900,000. Of that large amount, $100,000 was given away immediately, and the remaining $800,000 over a period of years. The money was given to support the local synod, a summer camp, and seminary scholarships; to assist struggling congregations; and to develop special outreach ministries. This exemplary church had established a pattern of believing this is the right thing to do. It still thrives today."

Hoffman concluded, "Having been a staff person for fifteen years with the Evangelical Lutheran Church in America, I have never encountered a church that failed to thrive when the minister put his or her salary on the line. For me, and for other pastors, it was the right thing to do, without doubt. I would do it again in an instant."

Come, But Take Your Chances!

The Reverend Doug Scalise is minister of the Brewster Baptist Church in Brewster, Massachusetts, on Cape Cod. Articles in the newspapers frequently report the growing number of retirees on "the Cape," and how difficult it is for working families to find affordable housing. Yet Brewster Baptist Church is thriving, filled with people from all walks of life. The church has about 400 adult members and draws 550 people at worship on Sundays.

"When I came here seven years ago," Scalise commented, "I sent a sermon in advance that was titled 'Museum, Mausoleum, or Mission.' I had no intention of presiding over a quiet church, and I was very clear about that. I actually didn't think they would call me. At the time, the prevailing attitude was, 'we don't want to do anything that might get us in trouble.' "

"I felt God was calling this church to be something greater than it was," Scalise continued, "and I knew we would never accomplish that with a single pastor. If we wanted to follow the will of God, I believed God would provide the resources. I believed that if we hired capable, outgoing, and faithful ministers, these good people would draw others to the church. That is what we did."

"The church hired an associate pastor even though we only had enough money for six months of salary," Scalise continued. "The leadership of the church took a deep breath when we did this, because the money was just not there. We didn't know how it was going to work out, but this was the direction we wanted to go. My firm belief is that churches will almost never have all the money they need to begin new ministries, but you can't wait until you have everything you need to get started. Churches have to step out in faith."

"I believe that in leadership, you lead. The minister's job is to equip and empower leaders and support them with energy, enthusiasm, and direction. Strong leadership gets things going. In turn, I promise a high-expectation church. You don't call your boss and say you're sleeping in, and you don't do that with God, either. We will not experience God if we live disobediently. A significant part of that is tithing, sharing in good measure what we have been given. Churches have a responsibility to encourage parishioners to give, and for the right reasons."

"In a surprising way," Scalise concluded, "we are a low pressure church. We don't encourage people to join until they're ready to make a commitment. That's what makes this a strong church. We'll need another $50,000 this coming year and I have no idea where that money will come from, but it will show up. I've been in the ministry for sixteen years, and it always has."

Exceptional Talent

Readers might conclude that these ministers were tremendously gifted in guiding their churches. Yet during interviews with these ministers, neither viewed himself in that manner. Each looked upon his work as helping people lead lives of faith that have intention and purpose. The Reverend Hoffman referred to this as "living faithfully," while the Reverend Scalise spoke of "not living disobediently." They believe that if this fundamental premise is in place, the congregation will fulfill its calling.

When I received a letter in the mail from the Reverend Scalise, I was pleased to see at the top of the letterhead stationery the phrase, "The adventure of a lifetime begins here." I believe people are instinctively drawn to a church (of whatever faith) that reflects the presence of God and invites them into a new way of life.

At Times, Church Is Counterintuitive

In the same way that churches take leaps of faith, I sometimes encourage churches to engage in practices that might be considered counterintuitive to good business policies.

Lyle Schaller describes this aspect of church life clearly. Along with his observation that healthy congregations respond to new challenges in ministry even when the money is not in hand, Schaller lists other criteria of a healthy church. These include:

—A strong future orientation

—Venturesome and risk-taking clergy and lay leaders

—A larger than average share of money given to mission, outreach, and community ministries.

His conclusion is the most extraordinary—that "highly successful churches encounter two to five financial crises every year, year after year."[1]

Readers may react in disbelief to this state of financial affairs in the church. The budget may not always be in balance. Expenses may exceed income. Parishioners may feel they are continually asked to give more money, or be worn down by the constant uncertainty of it all. Schaller himself concludes with the comment "For some reason that is difficult to explain, rational, logical, and thoughtful observers have difficulty comprehending why [this] appears to be an essential component of that entire scenario."

The opposite of healthy churches are those that Schaller describes as having an orientation to the past, leaders that withhold approval rather than grant permission, an atmosphere of caution, and a surplus in the treasury at the end of the year.

I sometimes think Schaller's formula is beyond my own ability as a generally rational, reasonable person to consider. Board members may wonder if they would be liable for financial decisions that didn't yield the intended results. As we have discussed, the issue is the level of financial risk the leadership and the congregation is willing to take, and the courage to take a leap of faith at opportune times.

Churches that display an attitude of hesitancy and caution might consider smaller risks first. These include projects in which the church has money available, as discussed in the previous chapter. These are ministries that can be modest in scope and shorter in duration. Projects like this have a greater chance of success, help build leadership, and create confidence in what congregations can accomplish when they set their minds to it.

Congregations don't have to jump into the deep end of the pool and engage in risky or large-scale ventures. Rather, clergy and lay leaders can dip their toes into the shallow end initially. But churches need to get into the water. A sad state of affairs exists in congregations that sit idly at poolside. Unfortunately, in my experience, all too many churches fit this category.

Possible New Ministries

The following is a list of ministries begun by congregations both large and small. These ministries range from simple, inexpensive initiatives like community gardens, to churches that started banks and large social service agencies. Many of these projects were begun on a shoestring budget by rank-and-file parishioners who witnessed sorrow, pain, and suffering in the world and wanted to do something about it. These examples are from Victor Claman's excellent book, *Acting on Your Faith: Congregations Making a Difference*.

—Providing a training program for people who will assist the elderly and homebound.

—Beginning an adult day program at a local health club.

—Setting up a program that allows children to visit their parents in prison.

—Sponsoring refugee families.

—Starting a bakery that provides job training and that gives away its baked goods to local food banks and soup kitchens.

—Providing a program that permits homeless people to have e-mail access and a mailing address where they can receive mail.

—Initiating after school programs for latchkey kids.

—Adopting a local school and providing volunteer time and money.

—Gathering a collection plate full of business cards—congregants who will help others find work.

—Supporting summer camps for at-risk youth.

—Starting a credit union for low-income people.

—Sponsoring Scout troops.

—Starting a program that helps recent immigrants deal with public agencies.

—Beginning "Taking It to the Streets," a program in which as many as 150 people walk the streets together in high crime neighborhoods from 9:00 P.M. to 1:00 A.M. on Fridays and Saturdays.

—Developing a partnership with an ethnic church, allowing the opportunity to worship together in each other's buildings.

—Organizing Habitat for Humanity house building trips for both adults and youth.

—Offering classes in English as a Second Language (ESL).

—Starting athletic teams for children, youth, and adults.

Two Critical Issues

A paramount issue in creating congregations willing to take leaps of faith is instilling a sense of "opportunity calling" within the congregation. This is the view that charitable giving is a means to ministry and service, not paying the church's bills.

Churches need adequate resources to take advantage of opportunities for ministry when they arise. The key concept is having *available* resources that can be leveraged at a moment's notice. I believe the freedom that comes from having an adequate balance in the church's checkbook creates adventuresome congregations that continually seek opportunities to serve.

The second critical issue returns us to the most dramatic difference between mainline churches and newly formed churches. In new churches, authority is granted to individuals and not only groups. In studying both types of churches, Donald Miller writes, "The current form of community for Christians in many mainline churches is the committee meeting, a very poor structure for the type of nurture and care that many are seeking."[2] The committee structure, as we have noted, also requires people to seek permission from numerous levels of administration, and frequently results in permission being withheld.

In contrast, newly formed churches empower lay leaders to create needed ministries. Examples abound. Miller writes

> There are groups for parents raising teenage children, those battling drug or alcohol addictions, people recovering from divorce, couples seeking advice on financial management, sports teams, parents investigating home schooling, and more. There is also a full range of men-only and women-only meetings, marriage renewal weekends, family camping outings, movie nights for teenagers, and activities for preteens. What is surprising is how quickly these churches develop a broad range of ministries in response to the spiritual as well as personal and recreational needs of converts.[3]

William Easum and Thomas Bandy helped define this approach to active ministry. Easum wrote about the "permission-giving church."[4] Bandy has provided a very instructive view of the difference between what he calls the traditional church and the thriving church:[5]

In the traditional church, people are	In the thriving church, people are
Initiated	Changed
Enrolled	Gifted
Informed	Called
Supervised	Equipped
Kept	Sent

I believe mainline churches should consider revamping the traditional committee structure and seek ways to empower lay leaders toward creative ministry. As we have noted, the team concept rather than the committee structure is one approach. Some mainline churches have formed what are sometimes referred to as "Small-group ministries," which provide groups within the church a closer sense of community and prayer, and encourage them to pursue their hopes, dreams, and service within the context of the church's mission.

I like the title of the article "Extremists, Radicals, and Nonconformists: Please Be One!"[6] In this article, author and minister Roberts Liardon wrote, "God never calls you to be average. Average is a mixture of good and bad. Nowhere in the Bible did God call anyone and keep them average. Instead, they built an ark in the midst of chaos; they parted the sea; they marched around walls, causing them to fall; they walked on the water; and people were totally healed as their shadow passed by."

We may not achieve such dramatic results today. But potential miracles are many when people of faith gather together and are set free in God's name. I believe all churches have this capacity.

CHAPTER EIGHT

The Cost Versus the Value of Professional Leadership

Many church people, without blinking an eye, will argue that clergy should not be adequately compensated or housed, while they assume a higher standard and would not settle for less.

The Reverend James McPhee, The United Methodist Church

Dudley Rose is an ordained minister in the United Church of Christ and a member of the faculty at Harvard Divinity School. Earlier in his career, he considered a job as pastor at an idyllic New England church, a picturesque colonial building perched on a prominent site in a mountainous area. The church had an endowment and adequate funds for ongoing operations. Rose, however, was taken aback at the low salary being offered. He asked the chair of the search committee, "Does the salary reflect the value of ministry, or is the salary a budgetary decision?" The gentleman replied, "The salary reflects the value of a minister." Rose responded, "Then I am not your pastor."

Recently, a minister showed me a worksheet provided by her denomination. This worksheet allowed ministers to break down the compensation package into various components—salary, housing, health care, pension. The bold heading at the top of the worksheet was "Total Cost of Ministry."

I felt a more appropriate title should be, "The Value of Professional Leadership to the Congregation," or perhaps, "The Congregation's Investment in Leadership and Its Future." All too often the prevailing attitude in church, as we have seen, is one of how much things cost, or more likely, how little can the church spend. Unfortunately, this attitude can begin with the salary of the minister (and other church staff, as well).

The view of "how much does the minister cost" perpetuates the notion of clergy as salaried employees rather than spiritual leaders who bring potentially greater value to the church and the larger community. (What was the value of the ministry of Martin Luther King Jr., in comparison to his compensation?) What is the value of a minister who may be the first person called in a family crisis? What is the value of a minister who presides over weddings, memorial services, and other memorable experiences in parishioners' lives? What is the value of a minister who encourages a congregation to address social and economic injustice in the community, and changes countless lives for the better? Yet denominational officials report that phone calls from search committees often begin, "We're looking for a new minister. What's the going rate these days?" Cost comes first, while the demands of the job and the minister's value to the congregation play a secondary role at best.

But First

This chapter pertains to mainline faiths, but once again, we need to contrast established denominations with independent churches. Newly formed churches use dramatically different ways to organize and staff a church.

For example, mainline churches tend to be structured on the model of a senior minister with a three-year seminary degree who serves as a generalist. This is rarely the case in independent churches. Ministers in newly formed churches may not be divinity school graduates, and in fact might believe that the longer a person is in seminary, the less likely he or she will be an effective church leader because other ministers become the peer group rather than parishioners. Ministers in newly formed churches might also believe that traditional seminaries are geared toward the established church, an institution that holds little promise for the future.

More than likely, the new church minister served in a larger church that provided specialized training for people to serve elsewhere as senior pastors. That new minister's primary skills are likely to include the specific skills of evangelism and church growth.

New churches realize the value of specialized skills to operate a church whose basic construct is constantly changing to adapt to current times. These churches have altered the language of the church world in a significant way due to the need for increasingly specialized staff and volunteers. For example, job titles are instructive and include:

Worship Pastor

Minister of Spiritual Formation

Dean of the Learning Community

Minister of Health

Minister of Discipling

Minister of Stewardship

Minister of Recreation

Director of Training

Church Planter

Minister of Missions

Minister of Preaching

Director of Ministries for Families with Young Children

Executive Pastor

Pastor of Living Skills

Director of Ministries for Families with Teenagers

Minister of Prayer

Gone forever in the new church are the traditional senior pastor trained as a generalist in seminary, an associate pastor similarly trained, a director of Christian education, and an organist or choir director. Staff roles are not "offices" with unchanging job descriptions, but rather more fluid roles that change as the church grows and changes.

For now, let us return to mainline denominations. Of particular interest is the issue of clergy compensation.

Limiting Factors in Compensation

Mainline denominations tend to perpetuate the "minister as employee" mentality by conducting salary surveys and publishing compensation guidelines. These guidelines are usually determined by seemingly commonsense factors: the job (senior, associate, or assistant minister), the size of a congregation, the annual budget, an allowance for regional economic differences (usually small), and years of experience in ministry. I believe this widespread practice inadvertently depresses clergy compensation and makes it difficult for ministers and congregations alike to negotiate salaries that are truly equitable.

Denominational officials often claim that compensation guidelines result in salary increases for clergy. If so, the main reason is that salaries were low to begin with. One denomination recommends a base salary for a minister with a three-year seminary degree of $24,165; another recommends $25,700. One denomination recommends adding $100 to the base salary for each year of experience. How many people in professions requiring a three-year graduate degree would accept such a low entry salary and the provision that a year of experience is worth $100?

In one denomination, 40 percent of ministers still work below the recommended salary guidelines. This is considered significant progress over the previous level of 60 percent below guidelines a few years before. One denomination's guidelines include a "15 percent below standard," "standard," and "15 percent above standard" scale. Would any of us wish to be placed in the 15 percent below standard category, which implies a substandard level of skill and ability? These guidelines do not state how many years it takes for a "below standard" minister to achieve the status of "standard." Some might view becoming "standard" as not exactly a great leap forward.

Not all denominations use the same criteria, and precise comparisons are difficult to make. Some denominations have more generous pension, insurance, and retirement benefits than others. Comparing compensation data from different denominations is not an exact science. However, common themes include minimum-level salaries and language that devalues the profession of ministry.

Supporting Evidence

Matthew Price is former director of the Pastoral Leadership Project at Duke University and current director of analytical research at the Episcopal Church Pension Group. In an article titled "Fear of Falling," in *Christian Century* magazine, he articulates how desperate the state of clergy compensation is today.

Price's analysis indicates that "ministers like to think of themselves as members of the middle class, but they are hanging onto that class by their fingernails." No longer can ministers assume, according to Price, "gradual income growth that most Americans with graduate degrees take for granted."

His conclusion is that "clergy today worry about how to pay off educational debts, finance a child's college education, purchase a home, and save enough for retirement—all hallmarks of a middle-class life. Compounding this predicament is guilt. Why must clergy be preoccupied with career moves and money when they have responded not to a career, but to a call?"[1]

According to a survey of 600 ministers conducted by the Barna Group in the summer of 2000, senior pastors with seminary degrees serving Protestant congregations receive an average compensation package including salary, housing, and benefits of $42,083. All ministers taken together earn an average of about $38,000. While these figures represent a 2 percent increase each year since 1992 because of inflation, Protestant senior ministers now earn less in terms of purchasing ability than a decade ago.[2] Can denominations truly claim that compensation guidelines have worked?

Ralph Mero is a denominational official who works in the field of clergy compensation and finance. In a telephone interview, he said, "It used to be that ministers earned about the same as college professors, and enjoyed similar status. Now, ministers' salaries are more in line with schoolteachers, nurses, and mid-level government employees. Their status has declined likewise."

Let's take a look at other guidelines that limit clergy compensation. A prime example is the rule that no minister can be paid more than three times the salary of any other minister in a particular geographic area. Thus, the most highly skilled minister in the largest church may find that his or her compensation is calculated in proportion to the least skilled minister in the smallest church. In no other profession does such a formula exist.

A second guideline from a different denomination states that the monthly housing allowance will be 1/100th of the median price of "reasonable" housing in a particular area. For example, if the median price of a reasonable house is $100,000, the maximum housing allowance is $1,000 monthly. But what if the minister has a sizable family, wishes living space for aging parents, desires to set up a home office, or would like to live in a nice neighborhood within walking distance of the church, and thus requires "unreasonable" housing? Does this put the minister in an awkward situation in regard to the stated guidelines?

Other compensation guidelines may be well intentioned but are based on faulty premises. These include the common practice of ministers starting out by being paid the minimum amount on the salary scale. I have seen job notices on bulletin boards seeking assistant ministers for as little as $18,000. These are full-time jobs. The assumption is that a newly minted minister will begin his or her service with a small church, and that small churches have little money and pay low salaries.

Yet I am familiar with many small churches that have considerable sums of money, or are located in affluent neighborhoods. These churches could easily pay more than the recommended salary. Most do not because they refer to denominational salary guidelines and select the lower figure. Skill, ability, intelligence, experience, and integrity are essential as qualifications for clergy, but these attributes do not seem to be factors in determining adequate compensation. Salary surveys and denominational guidelines have a "lowest common denominator" effect on clergy compensation. Denominations, lay leaders, and ministers themselves have bought into a system that emphasizes the lowest possible cost of ministry, and not the greater value that a minister and clergy family brings to a religious community.

Compensation guidelines also mean that a mediocre minister may be paid the same as one who is a true spiritual leader, if they happen to work in churches of comparable size. The only way that a stellar minister can earn more is to move to a "taller steeple" church. But what if that minister believes his or her calling may be in a small or midsized church?

What if excellent ministers do not wish to live in large metropolitan areas where higher-paying churches are usually located? Rarely mentioned is the option of a smaller church being encouraged to pay above recommended salary guidelines. While some guidelines suggest that congregations are not bound by the figures, this is often included as an afterthought, and few churches pay more than the recommended salary levels.

It bears repeating that compensation guidelines are most often based on the size of the congregation and the annual operating budget. But what about the two hundred member church in an affluent suburb with an endowment of $3 million versus a church of similar size in the inner city with no endowment? Are these ministerial roles comparable? Should compensation for the minister in these two churches be calculated using the same formula?

What about churches of the same size that have troubled histories versus churches in which there is strong lay support and a high regard for ministry? Are these two clergy jobs so similar that they are compensated equally? Would not these two jobs be dramatically different in the demands they present?

What about churches that are growing in membership versus those in decline, that by coincidence have the same membership and annual budget? Are these ministerial jobs comparable?

Churches vary considerably in the demands they present to religious leaders. Individual minister's circumstances also vary. I do not believe that one standard, based on questionable criteria, should apply to churches and ministers across the board. I believe denominational guidelines perpetuate a "one size fits all" mentality with an emphasis on minimum compensation levels.

One denomination's guidelines do contain a single sentence that recommends congregations take into account the demands of the job. However, this is a fleeting reference, and no further guidance is provided to determine what these demands might be.

We might contrast this long-standing practice in Protestant denominations with that of our Jewish counterparts. In some Protestant churches, the belief is that the minister should be paid no more than the parishioner who earns the least. After all, clergy are called to spiritual, not material gain. They are to follow the sacrificial ideal of Jesus. However, in some Jewish synagogues, the rabbi's compensation stands in stark contrast, being determined on the basis of the highest-paid congregant. Many rabbis enjoy six-figure salaries, and their status in the community is comparable to highly compensated physicians, attorneys, and other skilled professionals. The issue is not a matter of salary alone, but the role the clergy family will play in the community. In many communities, members of the Jewish synagogue are similar in socioeconomic status to those of Protestant congregations just down the street. What a difference a culture makes!

The Minister Is Left Out

The missing ingredient in the salary formula is the minister, who has little role in determining his or her compensation. The compensation "package," which includes salary, housing, benefits, professional expenses, health care, and pension, is usually set by a congregation in advance. There is little possibility of negotiation, even if the church has the money. If the minister questions the salary, he or she can be perceived as playing "hardball," which is considered inappropriate.

The "package" approach of salary, housing, and benefits added together also works against adequate clergy compensation. Parishioners frequently perceive the total package as salary alone, no matter how many times it is explained otherwise.

All too often in seeking a minister, a search committee simply refers to the appropriate category on the denomination's chart for a salary figure. Congregations should take the time to evaluate in depth the true demands of the ministerial role, the respect the minister should have in the community, and the congregation's ability to provide adequate compensation. Is it appropriate for the minister to be underpaid and undervalued when the church holds significant assets? True religious leadership must emerge here. If a congregation decides the minister should be paid twice the recommended salary, so be it!

I believe the compensation discussion should be directed away from dollars and cents on the salary scale and toward the experience of the clergy family. For example, one denomination calculates clergy compensation based on salary and benefits data from private industry and government, along with salary ranges used by other denominations. While the survey approach yields compensation data, it does not represent the experience of the clergy family. Ministers are not employees in industry or government. A call to ministry is vastly different from a career in the private sector, and it involves a wider range of issues—in particular the clergy family.

Appropriate Measures in Determining the Minister's Compensation

Following is a list of questions that are often overlooked when determining the minister's compensation.

If there is not a parsonage, will the minister's compensation allow the clergy family to purchase a home in the community in which the church is located?

If so, will that home be in a section of town in which an "average" parishioner lives, or will it be in a less desirable neighborhood?

If there is a parsonage, is this considered "free" housing, a benefit to the minister instead of to the church? If the minister lives in a parsonage, does he or she receive an equity payment that is comparable to the gains historically realized through home ownership?

If the minister cannot afford a home in the church community, is it acceptable for the clergy family to live in a less expensive (less desirable) community?

If the minister lives in a less desirable community, is it acceptable for the clergy family not to be involved in the day-to-day life of the church community?

If the minister has children, is it acceptable for them not to be in the local school system? Is it acceptable for the clergy family not to be involved in the town's youth sports or artistic activities, and live their lives in a town separate from parishioners' children and families?

If the minister lives in a less desirable community, how long a commute is acceptable for daily work, evening meetings, Sunday worship, and other church events? Fifteen minutes? Thirty minutes? An hour? More than an hour?

Is it acceptable for the minister to drive a car that is noticeably older or in worse repair than the average parishioner?

Is the minister's spouse expected to work in order for the family to have an adequate income?

Is it acceptable for the minister to "moonlight," to take a second job in order to earn a living; or to conduct weekend weddings for non-members in order to make ends meet?

Is it acceptable for the minister to wear worn-out clothing because he or she cannot afford to buy new clothes?

Is it acceptable for parishioners to give used clothing, furniture, or children's toys to the minister and his or her family? Is the clergy family expected to be grateful for cast-off items that parishioners no longer want?

Is it acceptable for the minister not to attend concerts, plays, or other artistic, or cultural events that parishioners attend because ticket prices are too high?

Is it fair to expect a low-salaried minister to make a leadership pledge to the church in order to set an example for others?

Compensation is not the total dollar package, but rather the quality of life of the clergy family. What effect does an inadequate salary and anxiety about money have on the minister, the clergy family, and the minister's ability to serve the church?

Congregational leaders also need to assess the level of compensation that reflects respect for ministry. What compensation level reflects the demands of the job, the challenges of the position, the commitment required, and the assets of the church? As noted, ministers have declined in status and compensation. I am hoping lay leaders will have the courage and fortitude to reverse this unfortunate trend. Let's look at two clergy families to see how compensation has affected their lives.

The Experiences of Clergy Families

The first example is from a minister in a mainline church in a relatively affluent suburb of about 100,000 people. He said, "In my first ministry, the church was located in a town that was growing rapidly and undergoing significant change. The membership of the church grew during my six-year ministry, and during what turned out to be my final year, the pledge drive brought in $50,000 more than the year before. Some elderly members in the leadership were unhappy with so many new faces at church, and they voted to freeze my salary at $29,000. I left shortly thereafter."

He continued, "I now serve a church with a $2.7 million endowment, and my base salary is $36,000. I can't afford to live in this town, so I commute 45 minutes one-way. I recently brought up the issue of salary to one of the church leaders, a man with a salary well into six figures. His response was that if I wanted more money, why didn't my wife get a job? I reminded him that we have two children under seven years of age and that both parents working full time did not reflect our family values."

This minister concluded by saying, "I'm not talking about having a summer home or going on European vacations. I just wish I had money for my child's swimming lessons. My parents pay for those extras. I'm grateful to them, but I'm in my thirties. I still have a few years of seminary debt to pay off. I thought I would be able to make my own way by now."

When I asked him about his ministerial colleagues, he replied, "Few are satisfied with compensation."

An Excellent Return on Investment

A second example also comes from a minister in a mainline denomination. She said, "When I accepted the call to serve this church twenty-five years ago, I was one of a small number of women in the ministry. My salary as assistant minister in my former church was the lowest in the denomination. Upon arriving at my new church as senior minister, I discovered that the salary on my signed contract had been reduced by 10 percent because the finance committee decided the original amount was too high. What could I do? We had already moved."

"After renting an apartment for six months, we found a small house we could afford to buy. We didn't understand at the time how socially unacceptable it was to live in that part of town. Our son was the only child from the congregation who attended our neighborhood elementary school. I found out years later that parishioners were embarrassed by the car we drove and where we lived, because we did not represent the proper social order."

She continued, "We were able to purchase our modest home because the church had a housing fund due to the sale of a parsonage some years before. However, there were no provisions regarding the interest rate the congregation would charge a minister. The church made us a housing loan in the early 1980s when interest rates had spiked to about 16 percent. They gave us a 'bargain' rate of 10 percent. I suspect that church leaders who set the 10 percent rate were paying considerably less themselves for their home loans.

"After five years of church growth and successful ministry by any measure, we were falling behind financially. I mentioned to the church president that I didn't want to move, but was beginning to look for another church, solely for salary reasons. Shortly thereafter, I received a 25 percent salary increase. While I felt better about my compensation, the church always had the money to pay me adequately. They just didn't want to spend it, even to pay a minister who was serving them well. As the years went by, I would forgo salary increases so the church could add needed staff to an ever-growing congregation. Many ministers do this.

"When we sold our house nine years later and paid off the housing loan, the church treasurer reported at the annual meeting, 'The church made more money on the minister than any other investment in the last nine years.' Everyone laughed. I can't tell you how disturbing that was. We were struggling financially much of that time. We also found out that our $1,000 pledge in 1981 put us among the top ten donors in the church. I felt we were treated disrespectfully, especially by those who had considerably more than we did. I served that church extremely well for fifteen years, but from time to time I think back on how poorly my compensation was handled. My salary may have been within the guidelines, but I don't recall because there were so many other issues involved."

The Reverend James McPhee of The United Methodist Church describes this attitude as "churches seeking to pay as little as possible for a minister, and feeling like they got a great bargain. This is related to the lack of self-reflection concerning the clergy family. The bottom line is, how we use our money reflects our values deeply. In many instances, this is not good news for clergy."

Some congregations do offer ministers "loans" that are intended to be forgiven. In most instances, the minister(s) are required to pay income taxes on the amount provided but are not obligated to repay the principal. These loans help clergy pay off seminary debt, other accumulated debt, or various living expenses.

A More Appropriate Measure

John Payne is a minister in the Presbyterian Church (USA) and he told a story about assisting a congregation with a minister's compensation. This particular minister was highly regarded by the congregation but was thinking about moving to another church that offered a higher salary. Payne asked lay leaders what the median household income was in that particular community. At the time, the figure was $32,000. Payne asked the church committee if $32,000 was about "what it took" to live in this community. Committee members agreed this figure was about right.

Payne then asked the committee what the current salary and housing figure (comparable to salary) was for the minister. The response was "$18,000." In discussing the disparity in figures, Payne asked if any committee members could live on that amount. The response was that they could not. He then asked committee members how the minister was supposed to live on that meager salary, how he was valued in the eyes of congregants, and what respect the minister had in the community.

I believe the Median Household Income and Median Family Income, in this instance $32,000, is a more applicable guide to clergy compensation than figures set by denominations. The median figure is the midpoint of salaries (half above, half below) in a given community, and is usually considered to be "what it takes" to live in a given city or town. These figures are readily available at any public library (ask for census data), Chamber of Commerce, or local bank.

It is important to note, however, that the Median Family or Median Household Income should be taken in context. In some areas, household income may exceed $100,000; yet exorbitant housing prices require a sizable down payment for anyone wishing to live in that community. In cities and dense urban areas, the Median Household Income often includes a significantly larger and more diverse population economically, and that figure might be $25,000 or less. This figure is a composite of both wealthy and poor areas, and may not reflect the economic situation of any one particular church or neighborhood.

If the median income for the city as a whole is not an accurate guide, an excellent substitute is the median family income of the congregation. This can be determined fairly accurately with some reasonable "guesstimates" of what average household income might be. It is not difficult to estimate the income of various professions. Or lay leaders might simply ascertain among themselves the level of income required to live in a particular community and arrive at a close approximation.

Ministers, organists, and other highly skilled staff might take a cue from the world of professional sports. Top dollar is paid for top talent. Ministers should play a role in discerning their own value and worth—and not have it determined (and usually diminished) by the quadruple whammy of denominational salary scales, miserly fiscal policies at many churches, minimal giving among large segments of a congregation, and salary ranges that are not applicable to local economic conditions.

No business on earth would dare suggest, "We're going to create a first-rate company by paying the lowest possible salaries for staff, starting with the CEO." Yet this attitude is the norm in the church world. Many forces, alas, act to keep this tradition firmly in place.

Make Some Waves!

Instead of falling into the "what is the least we can spend" approach in terms of clergy compensation, I'd like to suggest a bit of mischievousness. Wouldn't you love to be part of a small- to medium-sized church that upended compensation guidelines and paid the minister more than the larger church up the street?

We did this in my church when hiring a youth advisor. National compensation guidelines recommended an extraordinarily low salary. Instead, we paid this advisor twice the going rate, based on his value to the church and the importance of his presence to our youth. This position was the highest paid youth job in the denomination, and our advisor subsequently won an award for youth advisor of the year. A number of committee members, myself included, raised our pledges to accomplish this, and it was great fun.

Believe me, if your church raises compensation levels for clergy and staff, word will get out. Such a bold step is also likely to ensure that your congregation will attract the top ministerial and staff talent available.

Acts of justice like this will address the desperate financial state of many clergy families and reverse the tradition of predetermined salary levels. Might your church be one of these beacons, leading the way? Would you not derive great enjoyment in belonging to a church that established a new order?

For readers who think that only large or wealthy congregations can do this, my experience is that affluent churches often display a higher level of anxiety about money than less affluent churches. With clergy salaries being so low, many churches could increase their minister's salary with ease. Churches often claim they don't have the money, but they almost always do. They just don't want to raise it, spend it, or give it. (Some readers may feel their ministers do not deserve a salary increase, based on performance. I believe low salaries dampen anyone's enthusiasm and attitude toward his or her work. How many people, in any occupation, strive continually to do their best when they are poorly paid and underappreciated?)

I often use a travel analogy to point out attitudes about the availability of money. Let us say I am a travel agent and call churches at random with a special offer of ten days in Europe at $1000 per traveler with twenty slots available. I suspect people would line up, cash in hand, to seize a bargain like this. If one of these same churches wished to hire a half-time staff person at a salary of $20,000, a chorus of voices would likely sing out, "We don't have that kind of money around here." The availability of money is rarely the issue. What people do with money is another story entirely.

Sometimes lay leaders will claim that salary guidelines are necessary because "we wouldn't know what to pay a minister otherwise." I do not think this is a valid excuse. Clergy should be compensated in proportion to their value and the demands of the job. Why can't intelligent lay leaders, sometimes bankers, lawyers, and financial advisors themselves, figure out on their own what constitutes decent compensation for the minister?

The Effect on Churches

Denominational guidelines not only limit clergy salaries, but also have a profound effect on church life as a whole. Human nature being what it is, people do not wish to pay more for something they can get for less. I am familiar with search committees that reduced the compensation package when seeking a new minister to save money they really didn't need to save. The reduced salary was not an arbitrary financial decision, but the next lower figure on the ladder of the compensation guidelines. The rationale for the salary reduction was, "Since the incoming minister may have less experience than our current minister, we'll go down one level on the salary scale." Of course, the expectations of the job were not reduced accordingly.

A similar salary construct applies to the American Guild of Organists. This issue became apparent in a newspaper article in a major city some years ago that listed the cost of a typical wedding. Included on the list was an organist who was paid $100 for the wedding ceremony, while a disk jockey for the reception was paid $600. Local organists were outraged at the gross inequity, yet adamantly refused to reconsider their salary structure.

Organists may view weddings as a pedestrian way to earn extra cash, but the salary structure perpetuates a commodity mentality. A consumer pays the lowest price for a commodity. The mind-set becomes "because they are paid the same, organists are the same." This creates a "lowest common denominator" effect, which lessens the value of the most skilled organists in the profession. This attitude, unfortunately, travels far beyond weddings and affects the role of organists in congregations as a whole. In my state, the hourly rate for an organist with a doctorate is half of what a plumber, electrician, or auto mechanic charges.

I learned recently that some ministers are charging 5 percent of the total cost of a wedding for couples who are not members of the church. In the Boston area, a minister collected a $1,600 fee using this formula. I believe this is a step in the right direction.

This reminds me of a story from the late 1970s, when the fee for a minister to conduct a wedding was $50 in the city where I lived at the time. A friend of mine came from a well-to-do Episcopalian family, and in midlife he went to seminary and was ordained to the ministry. He did not serve a parish, but conducted weddings and funerals, and was invited to preach here and there on occasion.

Early in his ministerial career, he was asked to conduct a wedding for a family friend. The mother of the bride said, "Would $1,000 be sufficient?" My friend replied, "That would be fine." From then on, he was paid $1,000 for weddings and funerals he conducted. This infuriated his ministerial colleagues who resented working for a pittance. My friend always responded, "The families believe I'm worth it, so why should I convince them otherwise? Why would I want them to think less of me?"

If the minister's compensation is inadequate, the congregation as a whole will be hampered in its ability to create a vital church. If the leadership of the church seeks a bargain in the minister, then most aspects of the church will be viewed similarly. As we have seen, low-level and same-level giving is the norm in many congregations. Inadequate compensation for the minister perpetuates this culture.

Sometimes I think the best thing that could happen in the church world is for ministers to band together and say, "My salary expectations are beyond what this church is offering."

Price Versus Value, from the World of Marketing

Harry Beckwith is a keen observer of price versus value in the secular world. He notes the concept of "the more it costs, the better it seems."[3] The price of an item creates certain perceptions. When we pay more for something, our expectations are greater and our level of satisfaction is higher. (The exception, of course, is finding a great bargain, maybe at the church rummage sale!)

For example, a diamond ring purchased from an upscale jewelry store with thick carpeting and elegant fixtures may carry a dramatically higher value in the minds of purchasers than the same ring bought at a discount department store. It is not just the ring, but the experience of purchasing, as well. Just being in an expensive store reflects our good taste and our financial ability to purchase an expensive item.

Beckwith argues that *increased satisfaction occurs even when an expensive item may be of lesser quality.* Thus, a smaller diamond from an exclusive jeweler may be perceived as having greater value than a larger diamond from the discount store. We add value when we pay more. We pay extra for style, cachet, or élan.

Barbara Ehrenreich raises this issue in her book, *Fear of Falling: The Inner Life of the Middle Class.* In a chapter titled "The Embrace of

Affluence," she quotes a stockbroker who said, "Many people don't want chain store labels on things they buy. Kenmore [the Sears brand of appliances] is a good name but not an upscale name. When they have friends over, people do not want these friends to see brand names like Sears or Kenmore. They want people to see names like Sony or Kitchen Aid."[4]

When it comes to what people are paid, Beckwith argues that the higher the "price," the salary, the higher a person's perceived quality. When we pay the most, we expect the best. We wish to be associated with the best. Ministers who are highly compensated are perceived likewise, conveying a heightened authority and expertise. Conversely, the lower the salary a minister accepts, the lower his or her credibility may be.

Low clergy salaries play into what Beckwith calls "the discount buyer." He writes, "You cannot build a lasting business on discount shoppers, and you cannot build a satisfying business and experience with them, either, because they do not value you and your work. In fact, in their continual efforts to get you to charge less, they are vividly communicating to you that your work is not worth to them what it is to you."[5]

We might translate this passage into the church world as, "You cannot build a lasting church with low-level donors, because they do not value the minister or the minister's work. In their continual efforts to pay low salaries and continually keep costs down, they communicate that the church is not worth to them what it is to you."

Beckwith then concludes his observation with the caveat, "Avoid the discount buyer." In my work with congregations, I sometimes believe that churches are the ultimate discount buyers. The attitude of "everything at the least cost, starting with professional staff," can be debilitating to religious communities.

I believe money should be viewed as an investment in creating a stronger church and a better world. Church should primarily be a matter of value, with cost being an issue that is considerably down the list.

People make charitable gifts to churches and nonprofit organizations that carry great meaning, importance, and value to them. In the world of secular nonprofit agencies, donors do not know the salary of the executive director. Most donors to nonprofit agencies have never seen the operating budget. They want to be a meaningful part of a meaningful organization, and charitable giving allows this.

Churches need to create and foster this attitude, beginning with more than adequate compensation for religious leaders. Parishioners wish for the church to be engaged in important and imaginative ministries. They yearn for credible leadership that will make the church a place of special importance in their lives. This does not come from the church being relegated to the role of the lowest possible bidder.

CHAPTER NINE

Your Congregation's Financial Identity, for Better or Worse

We've been having stewardship conferences in this diocese for ten years, and I don't think they have made much difference at all.

The Reverend Margaret Shea, Presbyterian Church (USA)

In this chapter, I ask readers to bear with me as I take a slightly circuitous route to the important subject of discerning a congregation's financial identity. I took this route myself before finding an effective way to address issues of stewardship and church finance that we've discussed in this book. The method I'll propose is one that I believe can truly result in systemic change in congregations.

Over the past few years, I was a speaker at numerous stewardship conferences, and a registrant at others. There always seemed to be something missing, and I questioned whether the recommendations I made in workshops, or the good ideas I heard from others, would take root back home. I would like to discuss stewardship conferences briefly, then propose an alternative that is geared specifically to the needs of individual congregations.

The Basic Model

The type of stewardship conference I'm referring to is a staple in the mainline church world. Usually, conferences are hosted by a judicatory or denomination for members of that same denomination. Nationwide nonprofit organizations also host conferences that attract a broader audience, including conservative churches. A third type of conference, for professional staff, is discussed later in the chapter.

Stewardship conferences vary in length, though the mainline variety is usually a one-day affair, often on a Saturday, hosted by a regional church. Sometimes, these gatherings begin with a dinner and keynote speaker on Friday evening. Conferences hosted by national organizations are more elaborate, are held at upscale hotels, and sometimes last three or four days. These gatherings include preconference and postconference events, tours, contemporary Christian music concerts, and outings to sporting events or theaters.

Speakers at local or regional conferences include preachers, authors of books about stewardship, people who have gained a reputation in some aspect of religious life, or sometimes a prominent person from outside the church world. Most often, the conference format is an opening talk, followed by a series of 60-minute workshops.

Denominational staff often lead these workshops, along with ministers and lay leaders whose churches have done well at stewardship or other types of programming. The more elaborate conferences bring in prominent speakers who may have a regional or national following. The conference fliers look appealing—some guaranteeing that giving will increase from 10 to 30 percent!

In balance, stewardship conferences do contain sparks of insight. Some speakers are knowledgeable about various topics and give stirring talks. I also believe great value lies in gathering people of faith together. One conference I attended was sponsored by four different denominations, and drew a varied audience. The atmosphere was festive and upbeat.

Unfortunately, much of what is presented at conferences will not have "staying power" back home. Let's take a brief look at why such gatherings are structurally ineffective.

What happens back home?

In most congregations, long-established patterns of skewed giving are the norm; that is, about one-third of congregants give about two-thirds of the money raised. I recall someone observing that churches are like mobiles, seeking their state of equilibrium once put in motion. This is all too often the result for well-meaning souls who attend stewardship conferences and return with the goal of increased giving in the congregation. Their efforts are likely to be moderately effective at best because the established giving culture in many congregations is so strongly entrenched and resistant to change.

Variations on a theme

One conference I attended had an interesting agenda, which included:

—One Size Does Not Fit All: Year-Round Stewardship

—All God's Children Got to Give: A Small Group Model for Increasing Generosity

—A Theology of Scarcity or Abundance?

—Stewardship: Reaching Out to the Generations

—Stewardship Through Planned Giving

—Sermons I Wished I Had Preached

This is an impressive lineup. Yet as I attended these workshops, I was struck by how similar they were in content—variations on a common theme. Much of what was presented had been in the literature for years. To be fair, some speakers were very good, and there were some bright moments. However, at the end of this daylong conference, I felt little was presented that would address systemic issues that limit stewardship in local congregations.

High turnover

Turnover on stewardship committees is perennially high, and those who attended a conference a year or two ago may have assumed other roles in church. It is now time for a new group to attend a stewardship conference. It is likely these newcomers will hear a message similar to that heard by the previous group. The workshop agenda for a conference held ten years ago may be surprisingly similar to one held today.

My experience is that mainline stewardship approaches don't vary that much over the years. Fund-raising techniques such as letters, fliers, and various themes-of-the-year are standard fare. Clergy and lay leaders claim these methods get stale, and they come to stewardship conferences seeking new ideas. Unfortunately, many workshops are variations on existing approaches that reinforce low-level and same-level giving among congregants.

Lack of a critical mass

A significant shortcoming of stewardship conferences is not the quality of the program, but the small number of people from any one congregation who can attend.

One of the most difficult aspects of church life, especially in small- to medium-sized congregations, is the sizable number of congregants who will be uncertain, ambiguous, uninterested, or opposed to initiatives the leadership proposes. Thus, a small number of people who were enlightened at a stewardship conference will face significant obstacles in influencing the larger segment of the congregation that stayed home.

It is extremely difficult, if not impossible, for a small number of parishioners to instill a fervor for stewardship into a congregation where that fervor does not currently exist. George Bullard is a keen observer of the church world, and his view is that 20 percent of the average attendance on Sunday morning is the number of committed people necessary to make substantive change in church.[1] You can do the math to determine how many people this would be in your church.

Conferences are discriminatory

Only people who are available can attend, which excludes large segments of many congregations. Those excluded tend to be younger working parents, who in many instances are the church leaders of the future.

At one conference, I asked a group of 150 people how many were born after 1965. Only one person raised her hand, and she was a denominational employee. With all due respect, those who are available to attend conferences may not be those who will lead effective stewardship efforts in their home congregations in the years to come.

Like minds

Conferences are usually sponsored by denominations or judicatories for their own members. Speakers and presenters also tend to be from that same denomination, or a comparable faith. This practice reinforces a limited range of traditional views. Stewardship conferences for mainline congregations exhibit mainline perspectives, and usually exclude ideas from other faiths (usually those more conservative, and always those non-Christian) that I believe should be taken into account.

What works in one church may not work in another

A common shortcoming of stewardship conferences is the "best practices" concept. This implies that what works in one congregation will work in another. In my experience, this is not often the case. Many practices are local in nature, and do not "export" well to other congregations.

All too often, "best practices" are mainly fund-raising methods. These include various formulas, pre-written letters, and "how we did it" events such as auctions, bake sales, car washes, dinners, and musical events. While these events can be fun and build friendships, many conference attendees realize these ideas would just not work in their own congregations.

Special event fund-raising does not create the true spirit of philanthropy. Often, dollar income is small in comparison to the amount of work required. More often than not, much of the work of special events also falls upon the women of the parish. In the world of fund-raising, a maxim is "The easiest way to raise money is to ask people for it. All other ways are more difficult." I wish more congregations took this to heart.

While special events gather people together and have value in the life of a congregation, they should not become a mainstay in raising money that members should have given in the first place.

Time constraints

Even the most brilliant speakers at stewardship conferences cannot possibly address the range of issues that parishioners bring with them. As we have noted, the giving culture of any particular congregation can be the result of decades if not centuries of history and tradition. A great deal of time and effort is required in order to analyze and accurately discern cultural patterns of individual congregations.

Given the complexity of congregational cultures, the 60-minute workshop format is barely sufficient to introduce topics, let alone discuss implementation in widely differing church settings.

For example, a church treasurer reported that a group of parishioners was withholding pledges because they were resentful that the new minister was being paid $5,000 more than the previous minister. What should the church do?

Another minister reported that her church has a $4 million endowment. She said, "I don't feel like I have a congregation, but rather a group of private investors." This congregation was low pledging, and worried about its stock portfolio decreasing in value. The church's finance committee believed its role was to minimize expenses, which it did exceedingly well. The minister referred to an article she had read titled, "Scrooge Would Feel Welcome Here," and said it applied to her church and its miserliness. What should she do?

A host of other questions arise that are also not on the conference agenda. Many involve personality issues. One minister spoke of a husband and wife team who were president and treasurer of the congregation respectively, and both held limited visions of what ministry should be. This pastor felt powerless to challenge their long-held authority. What was he to do? Conference participants often comment that they feel their congregations yearn for the future, yet they are shackled to the past. They wish to create more engaging congregations, but are thwarted by the limited vision of many in the church.

One minister said his congregation had adopted a deficit budget in the spring and had made the decision to ask parishioners for more money in the fall. Was this a good or a bad idea?

Other questions involve myriad frustrations that clergy and steward-ship volunteers encounter. These include difficulty in recruiting leader-ship, high turnover on stewardship committees, volunteers failing to complete assignments, haranguing people who do not return pledge cards, and stewardship committee members being disheartened by the seemingly intractable patterns of low-level giving among fellow parish-ioners. There are just no one-minute answers to these complex issues.

Sometimes at conferences, people from "tall steeple" churches give presentations about the hundreds of thousands of dollars they raise each year, or the millions of dollars raised in a capital campaign. While these are laudable tales, the magnitude of these grand churches can be intimi-dating to the majority of people who represent smaller churches, adding to the inferiority complex that many small churches already feel.

These are but a few of the representative issues that cannot be addressed in the traditional conference format. This is why conferences, even those with excellent speakers, are structurally ineffective. Workshop topics and the limited time frame just cannot explore complex issues in sufficient depth.

A Recommended Alternative

Denominations, judicatories, and church-related nonprofit organiza-tions should develop stewardship conferences that "go on the road." Using this method, knowledgeable clergy, lay leaders, and consultants would train interested and capable people who can visit churches and spend longer periods of time on-site with the 25 percent of congregants who constitute the leadership of most churches. I believe this is the only truly effective method of bringing about systemic change and addressing the financial and leadership issues that face congregations today.

The keys to successful outcomes are spending sufficient time on site, getting to know parishioners, building trust, and learning first hand about the particular issues a church faces. Once a requisite understand-ing of the issues is reached, those who are engaged in this kind of work can then define and address the complex aspects around money that con-front the congregation—and that constitute its unique financial identity.

Determining a Congregation's Financial Identity as the Basis for Systemic Change

It is my strong belief that no one should make any stewardship or financial recommendations to a congregation until the following elements have been taken into account:

1. There should be an understanding that all churches are unique, and that no prewritten, "off the shelf" formulas can be used. The task at hand is to draw out the direct experience of clergy, lay leaders, and members of the congregation, and to use the findings as the basis for a tailor-made stewardship/financial plan. Thus, no two plans will ever be alike. Each congregation presents new and groundbreaking opportunities for learning.

2. A significant amount of homework should be completed. This includes analyzing the last three to five annual reports, the giving figures for the past five years, membership gains and losses over the past five years, recent financial statements, the current operating budget, the expectations of membership in the church, sample newsletters, stewardship sermons, the figures from any capital campaigns or special appeals, and any analyses of financial data the church has done. Only from this extensive review can the church's financial situation be discerned.

3. Anyone assisting a congregation needs to interview by telephone the minister(s), church president, treasurer or chair of the finance committee (or both), chair of the stewardship committee, and chair of the membership committee in advance of any visits or meetings. If any of these clergy or lay leaders is new to the job, it is important to talk with their immediate predecessors. It is only through conversations with the leadership that a true portrait of a congregation's giving patterns and attitudes toward money will emerge. Be aware that church members' opinions will vary and may conflict with one another. In my own work, I request the e-mail addresses of board members and key

volunteers, so I can maintain an ongoing discussion as issues arise.

A consultant or denominational staff person should resist any church's request to "come and talk with us about stewardship" until these facts and figures are in hand. This includes the "tall steeple" churches. The larger the church, the more complex the financial issues will be. Meetings about the generic subject of stewardship without relevant data are almost always unproductive.

In my consulting practice, I charge a fee for an assessment of the church's data, phone interviews with congregational leaders, and the initial meeting. If a church is serious about dealing with stewardship, it will pay this fee without question. If the leadership is unwilling to make an investment in this initial work, that church is unlikely to make a commitment to address the issues they have identified.

Denominational staff who provide stewardship services at no charge because churches pay annual dues can face significant obstacles in doing this work. These obstacles include staff people being perceived as having low credibility because they are "free," last-minute cancelations of meetings, and few incentives for the congregation to follow up on recommendations made. Also, staff people are rarely provided the opportunity to spend sufficient time in any one congregation to address the range of issues identified in this book. Staff should be cautious, because the upshot might be, "We had Joe or Jane here, but they didn't really accomplish anything."

4. From the data collected, an agenda for a meeting with clergy and lay leaders can then be scheduled. The agenda will vary from church to church. For example, one church might have an endowment that has precipitated decreased annual giving. Another church may have a transient population, and have difficulty in developing leadership and commitment. Yet another church might be experiencing the commonplace situation of a smaller number of parishioners giving more, while a larger number give less.

Many churches, as we have seen, also have ambiguous expectations of membership and are vague about charitable giving. All are different, and the initial meeting should address key issues identified through the analysis of written materials, financial data, and phone interviews with the church's leadership. This initial meeting is not a "sit and listen" event. This is a working session devoted to the issues that have been identified. The responsibility for good work and an effective outcome is as much that of congregational leaders as the staff member or consultant.

5. In my own work, I prefer spending two weekends with a congregation. I meet with the leadership on Saturday to work through the agenda. I also attend worship services (and preach whenever possible) on Sunday morning, and take a period of time following worship to meet with as many members of the congregation who wish to attend. I encourage the leadership of the church to turn out a group of 75 to 100 people, which approximates the critical mass necessary to make changes in congregational life.

6. Following the analysis and weekend meetings, it is important to provide the church with a written report of the findings. In my experience, a ten- to fifteen-page interim report is sufficient to include both the analysis and a tentative stewardship plan. This interim report should be distributed to the congregation for their review and feedback.

7. I believe a return visit to the congregation is also important. This may include attending worship services once again and being available afterward for questions and answers. If the church's financial situation is complicated, a separate meeting with the leadership is also warranted. Following these conversations, the final written report can be completed.

Examples of Financial Identities

I have identified six different financial identities based on a congregation's assets and its level of anxiety about money. Admittedly, each church has a different history, tradition, and theology. The make-up of a church's parishioners also varies from place to place.

A congregation's geographic site is also a key element. For example, a church may have a small membership and operating budget, but be located in an expensive area of the country. Its property may be worth millions of dollars. Conversely, a larger congregation with a greater cash flow may be located in a less expensive area, and its property may be valued at a considerably lesser amount.

In the examples that follow, clergy and lay leaders will need to make some judgment calls about whether their church's assets fall into the high, moderate, or low category. This might be an interesting conversation in itself. Nevertheless, I believe most churches will fit into one of the categories below. These examples, along with a recommended stewardship/financial plan for each, will help clergy and lay leaders place their congregations in some perspective.

1. Churches with Large Assets

These churches often have sizable plants, multiple staff, and "big ticket" expenditures. Or they may be smaller churches with large assets accumulated through bequests and other major gifts. Churches in this category have combined assets in property and endowment of $4 to $10 million or more, sometimes in the tens of millions or hundreds of millions of dollars.

High Anxiety

Churches with large assets and a high level of anxiety around money often support a wide range of programs and services. Many churches with large endowments also support mission and outreach efforts through these funds. Some have established separate foundations to distribute money to a variety of causes.

However, the distinguishing feature of a church with large assets and high anxiety around money is often a power struggle over who controls the church's finances. Various factions can form and be in constant disagreement. An ongoing concern is that the church will run out of money, even if it has large sums in endowment. The tendency is to worry about the future, and the leadership may want to cut back rather than explore new opportunities to serve.

These churches sometimes exhibit a distrust of both clergy and lay leadership, and a sense that few people are in charge because so many people believe they are in charge. Per-member giving is likely to be low, with a large number of non-donor households.

Sometimes, visible hostility arises between various factions because dollar amounts are significant and, regardless of how money is handled, someone will be critical. Newcomers may be wary of a church like this, and if they join they are likely to involve themselves in nonfinancial and nongovernance aspects of the church.

If a culture of anxiety and mistrust has developed over a long period of time, it is likely to take a similar period of time to rectify. A key element is restoring a basic level of trust and confidence in the leadership. A quicker way would be for various factions to turn over their leadership roles to others, but they are unlikely to do so because they believe no one can replace them. Assistance from the denomination, a consultant, or other outside party may be necessary.

A tailored stewardship/financial plan will involve a close reexamination of the church's basic purpose—what God is calling this congregation to do in this place and time—and what the core values are regarding the use of money. Churches like this would benefit from a concentrated period of time devoted to addressing these specific issues, using sermons from the pulpit, discussion groups, visiting speakers, and articles and books on effective church communities. An important element in the high asset/high anxiety church is the congregation establishing its own identity and purpose beyond the church's accumulated assets.

Churches in this category might benefit from establishing a kind of "pass through" fund specifically for new ministries in the name of the congregation itself. This fund would be in addition to any money currently being generated from established accounts or endowments. This would allow parishioners to contribute in good faith to the church, knowing their money would go directly to good causes. I do not believe such a fund would jeopardize the annual operating budget. Generosity begets generosity. A church in this category needs to focus outward, away from internal struggles. By doing good works, a church will help heal itself.

Moderate to Low Anxiety

Theses churches may also have a large physical plant and operating budget, a sizable membership, a wide range of programs, and total assets of $4 million or more. Or, as mentioned, they may be smaller churches with sizable accumulated assets.

In these churches, someone in the leadership may be familiar with the work of Edwin Friedman or Family Systems Therapy, and recognize the importance of nonanxious leaders.[2] Or the church has developed a culture of faith and trust in God that financial support will materialize to achieve the larger mission. Earlier in this book, I provided examples of churches that gave away large sums of money and found themselves with more members and more money than they started with.

Very likely, these churches attract visitors and newcomers because of the congregations' reputation or credibility in the community and the world. The presence of God is palpable. These are churches about which parishioners tell their friends and neighbors, and they exhibit a considerable degree of enthusiastic evangelism. Per member giving is likely to be high, and there is sufficient money to run the church. The giving expectations of membership are likely to be very clear, including the encouragement to tithe.

These congregations place high trust in clergy and lay leadership, and many members may be uninvolved in financial decisions. This church may also have a history of long pastorates.

A tailor-made stewardship plan for this congregation would involve creating a climate in which newcomers are encouraged to aspire to positions of leadership. The current generation of leaders needs to ensure that younger generations will continue a significant legacy of charitable giving, outreach, and service. This church requires ever-greater challenges and adventuresome leadership that will take risks and reach out in new and imaginative ways to serve a world in need.

2. Churches with Moderate Assets

This church is the norm in the mainline world. Total assets, including real property, may range from $500,000 to about $4 million.

High Anxiety

Churches in the moderate asset range may also have a wide range of programs and services. Many programs might have been initiated years ago, however, and may have remained basically unchanged over time. Usually, there is more tension around money than need be. The membership is more or less stable, with occasional increases and decreases. The focus of the annual pledge drive is likely to be on the operating budget. The church can pay its bills, but the budget is usually "tight" and new initiatives are difficult to implement. The church may have some debt that it is paying down. This church also may have a history of short-term or moderate-term pastorates.

This financial situation is likely to put the church into the category of "permission withholding." The leadership may not approve new ministries because of an ongoing lack of funds. Staff may grumble about low salaries when they see the size of the endowment in the church's annual report. Church leaders may find themselves working in caretaker roles, rather than providing a compelling vision.

In regard to a stewardship/financial plan, these churches desperately need more adventuresome leadership, and they need to take some risks or leaps of faith. These churches need the tangible experience that if the Lord calls, the Lord will provide.

Integral to creating excitement and interest in new ministries is a permission-granting atmosphere, in which congregants can act on behalf of the church when they see pain and suffering in the world. A key to a congregation's ability to do this might also be a New Ministries Seed Fund, in which amounts of money are readily available for exactly that purpose.

I am familiar with one church that began holding a special pledge drive for new ministries in the spring, the opposite season of the fall pledge drive for the church. This congregation of about six hundred members now raises over $100,000 for mission and outreach each spring, and the annual pledge drive has not fallen off.

Many churches now give away the loose cash that comes in through the Sunday offering, either for outreach, or to add to the new ministries fund. As we have noted frequently, the capacity of people to give, and the availability of money, are rarely the issues. People need to give in order to be made whole.

Another congregation with which I am familiar took a somewhat different approach, not based so much on theology, but on inaction. The minister of this congregation said, "When the church called me as minister, they said they were tired of sitting around in groups talking with one another, and wanted to get out and do something!"

Low Anxiety
In these churches, annual costs are in proportion to the congregation's giving. This church may have a valuable asset in the church's property or land. Most likely, this church carries no debt. This may be the local, pastoral, neigh-

borhood church that everyone likes. It might be an historic church that was established long ago, and takes everything that comes along in stride.

This church may exhibit moderate to high levels of giving, and may have a long-term minister who has strong pastoral skills. A financial/stewardship plan might include encouraging the congregation to initiate new ministries, and challenging the membership to reach out in new ways. The tendency of the members of this congregation might be toward complacency, since things run so smoothly.

3. Low Assets

Churches in this category are likely to have assets of less than $500,000, some considerably less.

High Anxiety

Two churches fit this category. The first is the "new start" church. One example is the nondenominational "house church" founded by someone called to ministry. The success rate of such churches is small, and while members of this fledgling church may not worry about money per se, they are uncertain whether the church will thrive.

The second "new start" church is one begun by an established denomination. Mainline faiths ordinarily do not use the house church model, but seek property and a building instead. This might involve finding a completely new site and building a brand new church, or purchasing an existing church structure. Denominations often invest financial and leadership resources into a new church start, but there is always uncertainty about whether the church will thrive or not. A stewardship plan will involve high levels of membership expectations and charitable giving.

The other category of high-anxiety churches includes those in a survival mode. These churches have a low or a declining membership and not enough money to pay ongoing obligations. The congregation may be spending endowment to meet current obligations, and they may have pared back programs and reduced the minister and church staff to part-time status.

Members may wonder whether the church will survive, whether their building will be sold, or whether they will be merged with another congregation. Various denominational rules may apply to churches in this category that supersede decisions made at the congregational level.

The denomination's involvement may determine the choices a congregation in this category might have. One option is for the denomination to recruit a charismatic minister to revitalize the church, but a caveat is that current members may not be in favor of such a drastic change. I have known churches to die rather than change.

Low Anxiety

My colleague John Payne describes this church as a "chapel." It appears to be timeless, and its goal is never to grow or be anything else than it is now. Churches in this category may have a single "vocation" that draws just enough newcomers to keep going on.

These churches may have part-time ministers or a series of supply preachers. They may also have laypersons who have held leadership roles for many years, perhaps decades. This is the kind of church that might operate on a deficit most of the year, then in a few month's time, for no apparent reason, enough money will show up to carry the church through. This church may have no interest in a financial or stewardship plan.

In Sum

Though the challenges are complex and varied, I believe that in each of these churches, effective leadership is the key to the future. Clergy and lay leaders in the same congregation may exhibit different levels of anxiety around money, and if extra money does come in, sometimes even more than enough, it still may not allay some people's fears!

Moving Forward

I believe the assessment and planning process outlined in this chapter is effective because it is tailored to a congregation's particular circumstances. However, this method is not a magic formula that will magically cure the church's stewardship ills. A congregation's attitude toward money has been a long time coming, and it will rarely change in the short term.

Congregational leaders should also realize that building effective stewardship is a multi-year process. It is one they will find increasingly interesting and engaging as time goes by, and as issues of congregational life can be explored in greater depth. For most lay leaders, this will be a welcome relief from the tedious chore of asking people for money year after year.

Clergy and lay leaders, denominational staff, and consultants using this method can develop new materials and approaches that suit the particular needs of individual congregations, whatever their situation. My experience is that congregational leaders and people in the pews do their best work when they join together at the church on site. They call one another to higher standards. They argue and debate. They search for solutions. They seek to be a better church. This is the work that faith in God challenges us to do.

A Final Word

I would like to conclude this chapter by briefly noting one additional type of stewardship conference. These gatherings are for professional staff, which I believe are extremely important. These conferences attract the top talent in the country and are specific in workshop content. For example, ever-changing tax laws carry financial and legal implications for individuals and institutions. Denominational staff people and consultants need to keep abreast of developments to serve their constituents effectively.

Denominational staff people and consultants are the ones who should get on airplanes and go to stewardship conferences. Clergy and lay leaders should stay home, search for the best expertise they can find, arrange for these top-shelf people to come calling, put them to the task, and hold them to the highest standards!

Making the Most of an Endowment

The purpose of an endowment is to grow the church of tomorrow, not enbalm the church of today.

Loren Mead, Founder, Alban Institute

I recently visited a church and found myself involved in an extraordinary experience. A bishop from Romania was visiting, and he gave a moving account of the church's frightening persecution under Romanian dictatorship. Those perilous years included the capture and torture of religious leaders, seizure and destruction of religious sites, and an attempt to obliterate religious expression altogether.

The bishop conveyed the good news that rightful ownership of the main seminary, seized two decades earlier, had been returned to the church. As a visitor, I could readily sense that this congregation was honored to be on the bishop's itinerary.

The bishop also spoke about a modest, $1 million capital campaign that was underway. The money would be used to restore the main seminary building, which also housed the church's headquarters. The restoration of this building would add a significant measure of hope to a region of the world where the average income is about thirty dollars a month, and people work in fields with hand tools. The audience listened in rapt attention.

Since notice of the bishop's visit was short, the Missions Committee asked the church board to allocate $10,000 from the church's $1.2

million unrestricted fund for the restoration project. This church of 425 adult members, founded in 1854 and whose building was paid for when the doors opened, has never carried debt. It is located in an affluent suburb where the median household income is $105,000 and the price of an average home in 2002 was $685,000.

Readers may suspect what happened. Not a single board member supported the request. The reasons included that accumulated funds were being saved for a "rainy day," for "hard times," and that the money was "sacred" and could not be touched. Taking money from accumulated funds would also "set a dangerous precedent." One board member was scornful to the mission's representative who attended the meeting, suggesting that it was highly inappropriate for this request even to be made.

This decision regarding the use of the endowment brought to mind a story told by the Reverend Loren Mead, who believes that churches too often behave like banks rather than communities of faith in terms of endowment policies.

Mead tells the story of a church that had a fire in its sanctuary. While insurance covered the basic replacement costs, congregational leaders wanted to use a portion of the unrestricted endowment to provide a number of needed enhancements in completing the restoration of the worship space. The finance committee turned down this request, saying the money was being saved for a rainy day. Mead concluded this anecdote by observing, "The problem with saving for a rainy day is that it never rains!" I've also heard about churches not wanting to spend money on leaky roofs—because of rainy days that might lie ahead!

The proper use of an endowment creates perennial debate. Two prevailing views are saving because the money might be needed later versus spending unrestricted endowment because it can usually be replaced. Sometimes these two points of view are referred to as "savers" and "spenders." Many other views fall along the spectrum.

Henry Hansmann, a professor at Yale Law School and a specialist on the economics of nonprofit organizations, is an authority on the issue of endowment use. His view is, "Saving is worthwhile only if you have a better use for the money in the future than you have today. There is often no reason to believe this will be the case." He also believes that since incomes in the United States have been increasing for the past 350 years, we are in fact asking for money from those who have less and saving it for those who will have more.

Hansmann believes that if the proverbial visitors from Mars came to earth and looked at how large universities, nonprofit organizations, and many churches operated, they would think these institutions were primarily investment funds—with programs and services run on the side.[1]

The issue of "saving for a rainy day" is at the core of the debate about endowments. Supposedly, the money will be there for hard times. My experience with churches, along with Hansmann's experience in secular organizations, is that when hard times do come, the endowment is not used for its intended purpose—to ensure the vitality of the congregation. Rather, the church cuts back on programs, services, support of the denomination, supplies, and in some instances, staff salaries.

The reason for these cutbacks is to preserve the value of the endowment. Thus, the endowment looms larger than the health and vitality of the church itself. Much effort can be expended into preserving assets that might not be used for decades.

It bears repeating that this attitude often stems from transferring our views about personal finance onto the institution of the church. In planning for the future and our eventual retirement, we hope to accumulate as large a net worth as possible. We would not touch these funds unless an emergency forced us to do so. This is considered prudent financial management.

In churches, however, the more appropriate financial decision may be to invest a portion (small or large) of accumulated funds into new ministries that enhance the long-term health and vitality of the congregation. Investing in ministry today may be a much wiser financial decision than saving money for an unspecified use at an undetermined date in the future.

An Alternative View

I recently completed a stewardship assessment for a church that had no debt and a $1.3 million cash endowment. Its total assets were approximately $2.5 million. This church, like many mainline churches in the United States, is on a plateau in terms of membership and charitable giving.

Among other things, I recommended the church form a partnership with a large social service agency. Clergy and lay leaders in this congregation believed their mission and outreach efforts were piecemeal, and I recommended they focus all their volunteer time, effort, and money toward this one agency. In forming this partnership, I encouraged the church to make a gift of $250,000 to the agency from the endowment. I also suggested that within three to five years, in one form or another, the church would have the money back. The church is considering this recommendation and is likely to take this course.

This church's leadership recognized the detrimental effects of keeping large sums of capital idle for decades on end. They realized this practice had created a culture of low-level giving and complacency in the congregation. Parishioners believed they didn't have to support the church because of its ample bank accounts. Church leaders also came to the realization that taking interest income to subsidize the operating budget was probably the last thing the endowment's donors wanted the money used for. The generous souls of yesterday were supporting the miserly souls of today.

The widespread habit of using interest income from the endowment for current use is cause for great concern. This is especially the case in affluent communities. I recall a phrase from years ago that is little used today, that of the "kept man." This was a pejorative term referring to an idle man who lived off the money of a wealthy woman. Churches with sizable endowments that draw large amounts of interest income for the operating budget and thus allow parishioners to give less are "kept churches." Using money from the past in this way is a serious moral and ethical issue. (The exception is small congregations housed in large old buildings that require significant amounts of maintenance.)

A minister once mentioned that she grew up in a large, thriving Methodist church whose bylaws did not permit endowment funds to be accumulated for unspecified purposes. This church believed it was called to do God's work today, and that saving money for no particular reason was not part of the Divine Plan. This church also believed that others probably needed the money more than they did. What a wonderful example!

Kurt Staven of Groton, Massachusetts wrote a little poem about endowments (D.R.E. stands for Director of Religious Education). It begins:

> Each Sunday the minister preaches and prays.
> The D. R. E. plans and the organist plays.
> The sexton cleans up in the usual ways.
> And all of them do it for . . .

Free, free, everything's free.
We're fully endowed through the next century.
Free, free, everything's free.
There's nothing to pay for when everything's free.

Before making any decisions about spending endowment, it is essential to determine what is referred to as "donor intent." In the secular world of universities, symphony orchestras, art museums, hospitals, and other "big ticket" organizations, donors often make gifts to establish permanent funds. These include endowed chairs, scholarship funds, and other accounts that are intended to remain in perpetuity. By law, the principal of these funds cannot be spent. For example, some universities still have scholarship funds that were established in the 1800s for orphans of ship captains lost at sea. (Potential recipients are few, and some universities have begun to "de-capitalize" these endowed accounts for other use.)

My observation is that bequests and other estate plans often do not carry donor intent of perpetuity. When people die, their wills provide for "Old First Church." The language in the will is for the betterment of the church as a whole. The church may have added restrictive endowment policies later on, or put the money into a restricted account, but the donor's intent may not have been a fund in perpetuity.

A related example involves churches that place surpluses from the operating budget into endowment accounts. Money that is raised during the annual pledge drive is clearly for current use, and donor intent is unmistakable. These are unrestricted funds. I believe that putting a surplus from the annual pledge drive into the endowment is a clear violation of donor intent.

Many opinions exist about the use of endowment. My belief is that churches should not march in lockstep with traditional views toward the use of money that is entrusted to their care. Saving may be important, but funding vital ministries may be even more important. Spending money on ministries that serve others can also be celebratory and contagious. Congregations take great pride in what they can accomplish with the resources at their command.

The Cardinal Rule

The true measure of an endowment's value is the proportion of funds used for institutional maintenance, compared to the proportion used for mission and outreach. If a significant portion of the endowment is used to serve only current members, I believe this is a serious misuse of funds that were entrusted to the church's care.

Mark Hildebrand is the director of a denominational foundation in Indiana whose board has struggled with the "save or spend" choice. He often refers to the familiar passage in Luke 12:48, "From everyone to whom much has been given, much will be required." Hildebrand adds to that sentiment, by noting, "To whom much is entrusted, even more will be demanded." I agree with Hildebrand that policies encouraging the needless hoarding of money and attendant miserliness should not be part of a community of faith.

Concluding Comments

Many churches do not have endowments, but I strongly recommend establishing policies toward the receipt of bequests or estate gifts. Churches can receive unexpected bequests from people who were members or friends decades before and have not been heard from since. It is far better to formulate policies toward such gifts in advance, rather than have the church embroiled in controversy over how to use a sum of money that suddenly arrived at the doorstep.

Loren Mead has written a twenty-page article on the use of endowment, titled "Endowed Congregations: Pros and Cons."[2] Mead illustrates the "pros" by including issues such as:

—Somebody trusted you with his or her money
—Endowments open doors to wider ministry
—An endowment calls you to deal with it, to live with it in faith

A few of the "cons" include:

—Endowments can be complicated and hard to manage
—An endowment may cause congregational giving to go down

—Money to be managed can create conflict and take attention away from mission.

Beyond the pros and cons, Mead also includes a number of recommendations that congregations should consider regarding the proper use of an endowment. These include whether a church manages its own funds, engages professional counsel, or incorporates a separate board or foundation. Churches seeking advice and counsel in regard to basic endowment issues would be well served by considering Mead's views.

I would add to Mead's list the question, "How much is enough?" I am familiar with two churches whose endowments are in the $60 million to $100 million range. Both are highly anxious about running short. How much more would it take to make them comfortable?

Another article, entitled "Congregational Endowment Funds" by Gerald W. Bauer, adds a nuts-and-bolts perspective on how people can make gifts to a congregation's endowment. This article includes brief and readable descriptions of various trusts and other chariable giving vehicles.[3]

There are many reasons for churches to have an endowment, and as many reasons not to. In a seminar I led recently, one minister was sharing her experience in a church that was struggling financially. She said, "If only we had an endowment, we would have the money to do the things we want to do." Across the room, an elderly gentleman identified himself as the treasurer of his church and replied, "My church has a $10 million endowment, and it has just about ruined us as a community of faith."

Clergy and lay leaders need to make judgment calls about whether or not to accumulate endowed funds. These decisions will vary, depending on the nature and character of the church, its history, its outlook for the future, and the attitudes of clergy and lay leaders.

A Final Note

A final word to readers is the familiar admonition to be careful what you ask for, because you might get it. Money is sometimes viewed as the solution to a church's woes, financial or otherwise, as in, "If we only had the money, we could . . . "

In my experience with churches of many denominations, money all too often creates as many problems as it solves. The bottom line is that clergy, lay leaders, and people in the pews who represent all socioeconomic levels are capable of creating lives of faith and meaning for themselves and others. This is the first priority—helping people find God. Everything else will flow from that.

Notes

Introductory Quote

1. Victor Claman, *Acting on Your Faith: Churches Making a Difference* (Boston: Insights Press, 1994), 120.

Introduction

1. Robert Wuthnow, *Christianity in the 21st Century: Reflections on the Challenges Ahead* (New York: Oxford University Press, 1993), 196.

1. Attitudes Toward Money in Church, Alas

1. George Barna, *How to Increase Giving in Your Church* (Ventura, Calif.: Regal Books, 1997), 61.
2. Donald E. Miller, *Reinventing American Protestantism: Christianity in the New Millennium* (University of California Press, 1999), 11.
3. Lyle E. Schaller, *The Very Large Church* (Nashville: Abingdon Press, 2000), 136.
4. Barna, *How to Increase Giving*, 13.
5. Edgar Schein, *The Corporate Culture Survival Guide: Sense and Nonsense About Culture Change* (San Francisco: Jossey-Bass, 1999), xiv.

6. Ibid.

7. C. Peter Wagner, *Churchquake: How the New Apostolic Reformation Is Shaking Up the Church as We Know It* (Ventura, Calif.: Gospel Light, 1999), 264.

8. Schein, *Corporate Culture Survival Guide*, 13.

9. Ibid., 26.

2. Whatever Happened to Sunday?

1. Rosemary Radford Reuther, *Christianity and the Making of the Modern Family* (Boston: Beacon Press, 2000), 5.

2. Daniel Wolpert, "Seekers Needed," *Congregations: The Alban Journal* (Jan./Feb. 2002), 3.

3. George Barna, *Evangelism That Works* (Ventura, Calif.: Regal Books, 1995), 50.

4. George Barna, *The Second Coming of the Church* (Nashville: Word Publishing, 1998), 19-20.

5. Massachusetts Council of Churches, 14 Beacon Street, Boston, MA (617) 523-2771. E-mail: council@masscouncilofchurches.org.

6. Patricia J. Williams, *Seeing a Color Blind Future* (New York: Noonday Press, 1997), 21.

7. Charles E. Bennison, Jr., *In Praise of Congregations* (Boston: Cowley Press, 1999), 23-24.

8. Brian McLaren, *A New Kind of Christian* (San Francisco: Jossey-Bass, 2001), ix-xiv.

9. Wagner, *Churchquake!*, 64.

10. Miller, *Reinventing American Protestantism*, 109.

11. Ibid., 22.

12. Barna, *Evangelism*, 37.

3. Brother, Can You Spare a Dime?

1. Lyle E. Schaller, *Activating the Passive Church* (Nashville: Abingdon Press, 1991), 51-52.

2. Ashley Hale, *The Lost Art of Church Fundraising* (Chicago: Precept Press, 1993), 87.

3. John and Sylvia Ronsvalle, *The State of Church Giving through 1997* (Champaign, Ill.: empty tomb, 1999), 1-2.

4. Robert Wuthnow, *The Crisis in the Churches: Spiritual Malaise, Fiscal Woe* (New York: Oxford University Press, 1997), chapters 7, 8, and 9.

5. Thandeka, *Learning to Be White: Money, Race, and God in America* (New York: Continuum Press, 1999).

6. George Kinder, *Seven Stages of Money Maturity* (New York: Dell/Random House, 1999), 11.

7. James Hudnut-Beumler, *Generous Saints* (Bethesda, Md.: The Alban Institute, 1999), 12.

4. Making the Annual Pledge Drive Obsolete

1. Wuthnow, *Christianity in the 21st Century*, 193.
2. Ibid., 200.
3. Wuthnow, *The Crisis in the Churches*, 239.
4. Ibid., 6-7.
5. Peter J. Gomes, *The Good Book: Reading the Bible with Mind and Heart* (New York: William Morrow, 1996), 289.
6. Juliet B. Schor, *The Overworked American: The Unexpected Decline of Leisure* (New York: BasicBooks, 1991), 29.
7. Joe Dominguez and Vicky Robin, *Your Money or Your Life* (New York: Penguin Books, 1999).
8. Zondervan ChurchSource, www.zondervanchurchsource.com.
9. Kortright Davis, *Serving with Power* (Mahwah, N.J.: Paulist Press, 1999), 16-18.
10. Gomes, *The Good Book*, 306-7.
11. Martin Luther King, in a sermon to Ebenezer Baptist Church, September 1965.
12. *Generous Giving Newsletter*, MMA Stewardship Center, 1-800-348-7768, or www.mma.on-line.org. September 2001 issue.
13. Barna, *Second Coming of the Church*, 36.
14. Barna, *Evangelism*, 51-52.
15. Wagner, *Churchquake!*, 254-55.

5. Who Controls the Money?

1. Lyle E. Schaller, *The New Reformation* (Nashville: Abingdon Press, 1995), 84.
2. Thomas A. Bandy, *Christian Chaos* (Nashville: Abingdon Press, 2001), 77.
3. Ibid., 68.
4. Schaller, *New Reformation*, 84.
5. Lyle E. Schaller, *The Middle-Sized Church* (Nashville: Abingdon Press, 1985), 20-21.
6. Schaller, *Activating the Passive Church*, 52.

6. Limiting Ministry Through Fiscal Responsibility

1. Lyle E. Schaller, *44 Ways to Expand the Financial Base of Your Congregation* (Nashville: Abingdon Press, 1989), 31.
2. Dale Galloway, "What Will You Give Up to Move Forward?" *Net Results Magazine*, September 2001, 20.
3. William Easum, *The Church Growth Handbook* (Nashville: Abingdon Press, 1990), 14.
4. Emile Durkheim, *The Elementary Forms of Religious Life* (New York: The Free Press, 1995), a new translation by Karen Fields, xvii.
5. Greg Ligon, "Finding Models to Implement Change," *Net Results Magazine*, September 2001, 9.

7. High-risk Ventures

1. Schaller, *44 Ways to Expand*, 32.
2. Miller, *Reinventing American Protestantism*, 189.
3. Ibid., 14-15.
4. William Easum, *Sacred Cows Make Gourmet Burgers* (Nashville: Abingdon Press, 1995), 49-57.
5. Bandy, *Christian Chaos*, 19.
6. Roberts Liardon, "Extremists, Radicals, and Non-conformists: Please Be One!" *Spirit Life International* (Summer 1996), 2.

8. The Cost Versus the Value of Professional Leadership

1. Matthew Price, "Fear of Falling," *Christian Century* (August 15-22, 2001): 18-21.
2. Salary data available at www.barna.org.
3. Harry Beckwith, *The Invisible Touch: Four Keys to Modern Marketing* (New York: Warner Books, 2000), 77.
4. Barbara Ehrenreich, *Fear of Falling: The Inner Life of the Middle Class* (New York: Harper, 1989), 229.
5. Beckwith, *The Invisible Touch*, 85.

9. Your Congregation's Financial Identity, for Better or Worse

1. Bullard is director of the Hollifield Leadership Center and Lake Hickory Learning Communities on Lake Hickory in North Carolina. He publishes *The Bullard Journal*, an e-magazine about congregational life. Further information on Bullard's work is available at www.holifield.org.
2. Edwin Friedman, *A Failure of Nerve: Leadership in the Age of the Quick Fix* (Bethesda, Md.: The Edwin Friedman Trust/Estate), Fax 301-229-4305.

10. Making the Most of an Endowment

1. *New York Times* Education Supplement, August 2, 1998.
2. Loren B. Mead, *Endowed Congregations: Pro and Con* (Bethesda, Md.: The Alban Institute, 2001).
3. Gerald W. Bauer, *Congregational Endowment Funds* (Bethesda, Md.: The Alban Institute, 2001).